SLOTH

COLORING BOOK FOR KIDS

THIS BOOK BELONGS TO:

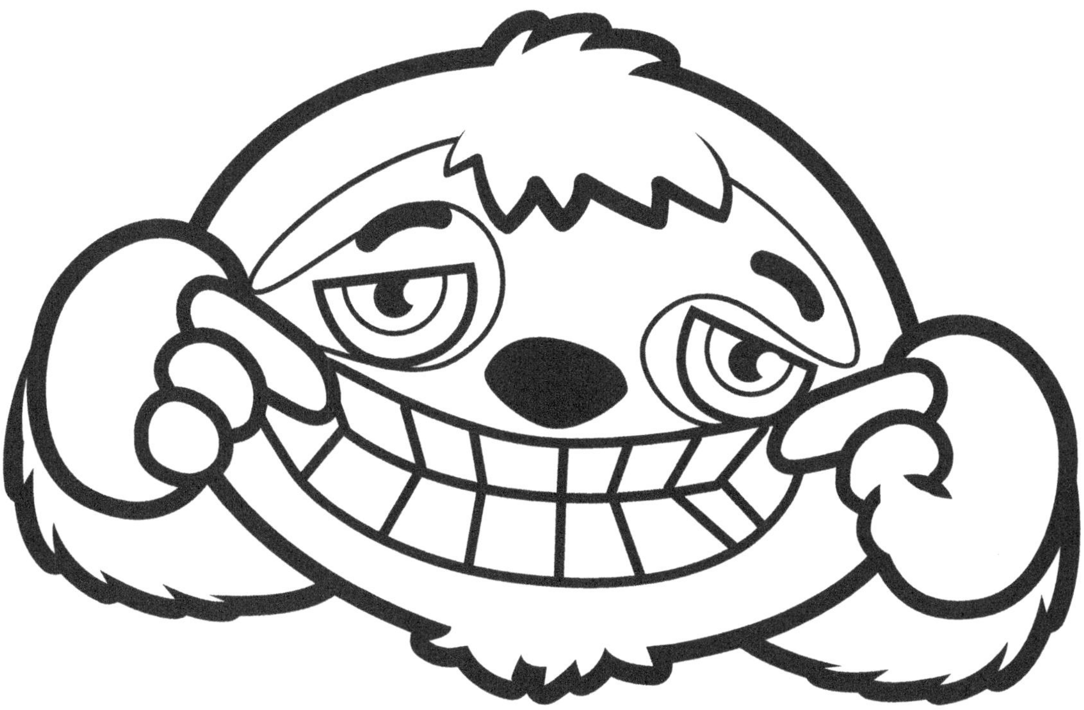

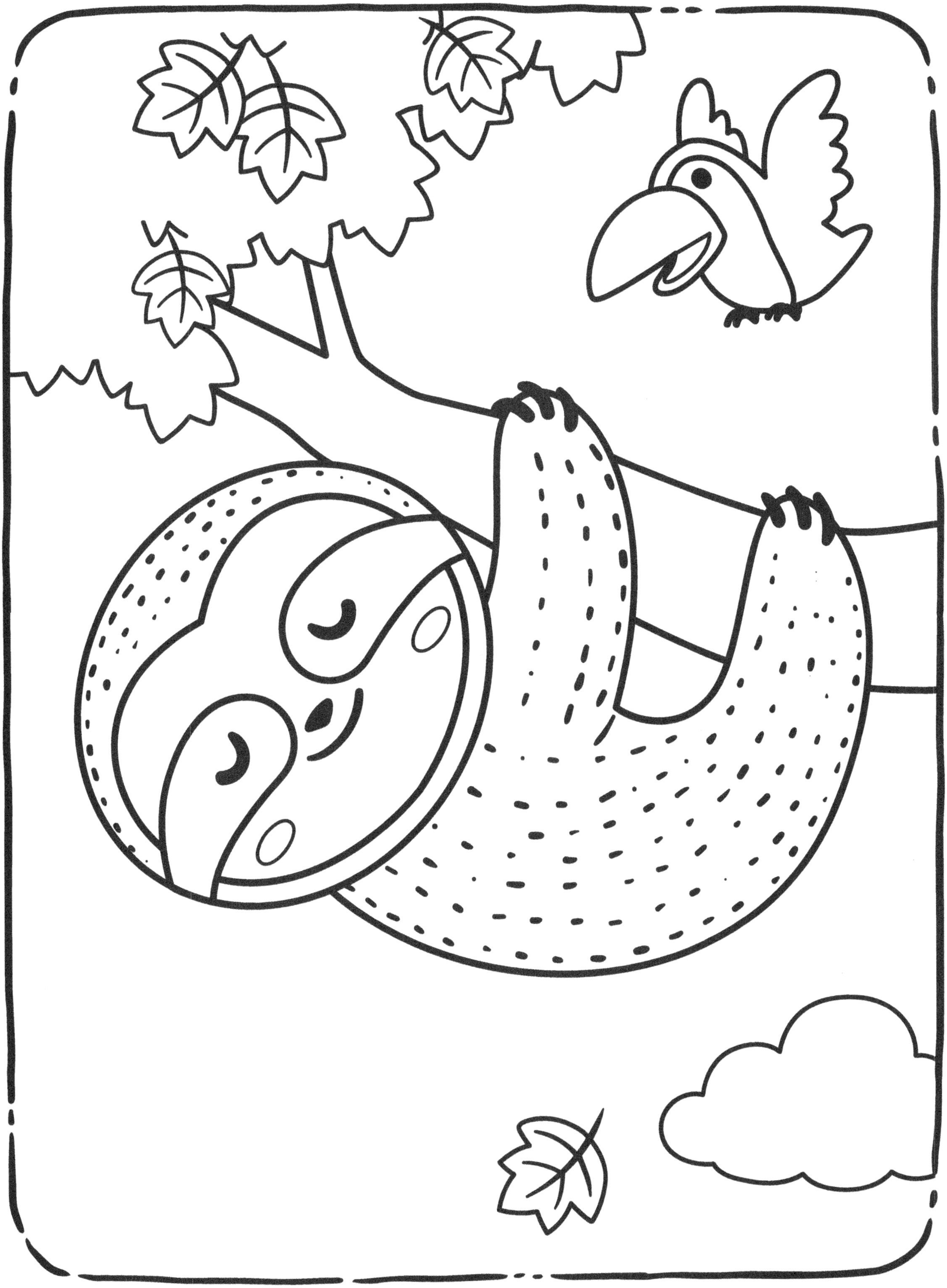

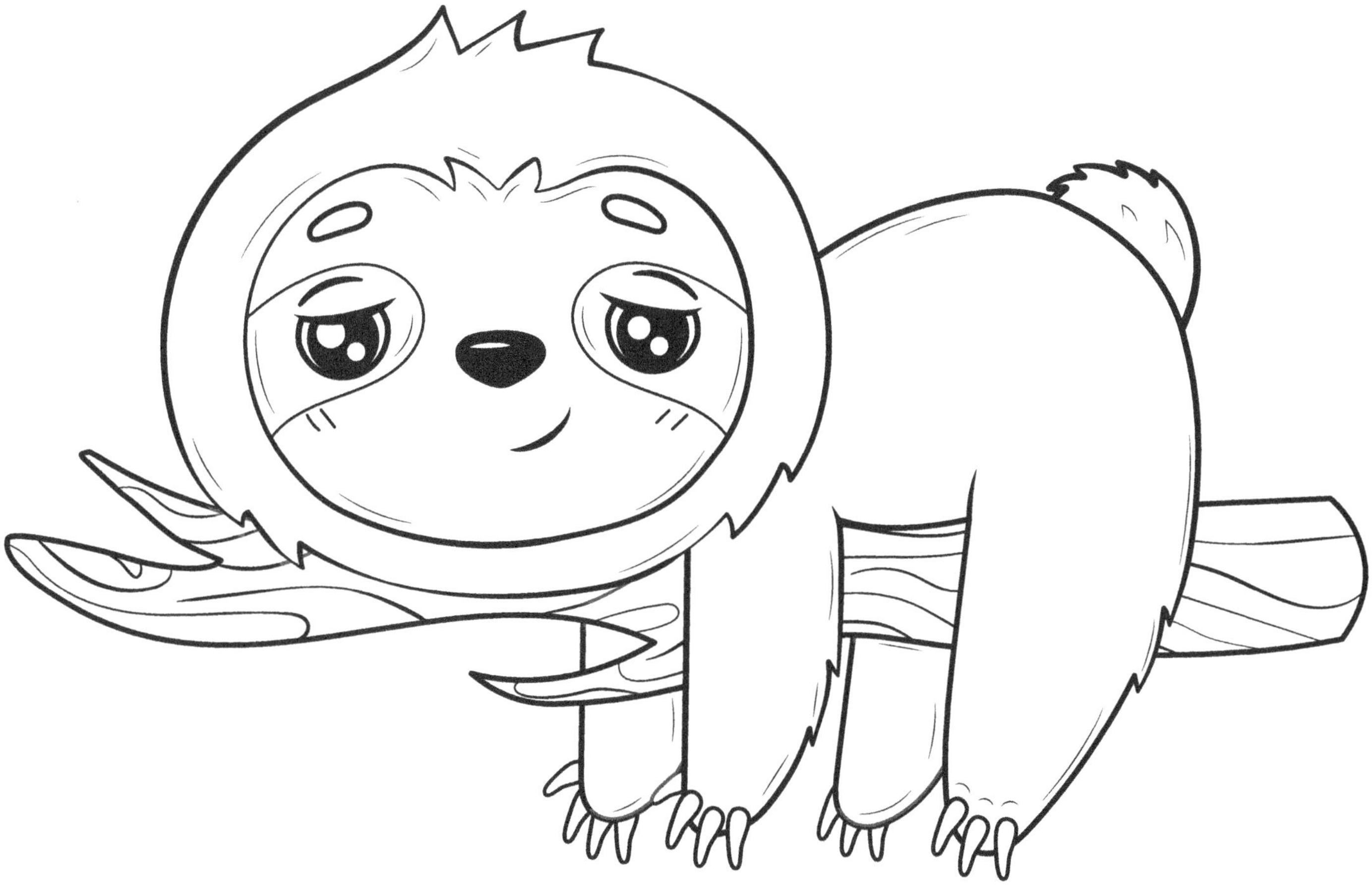

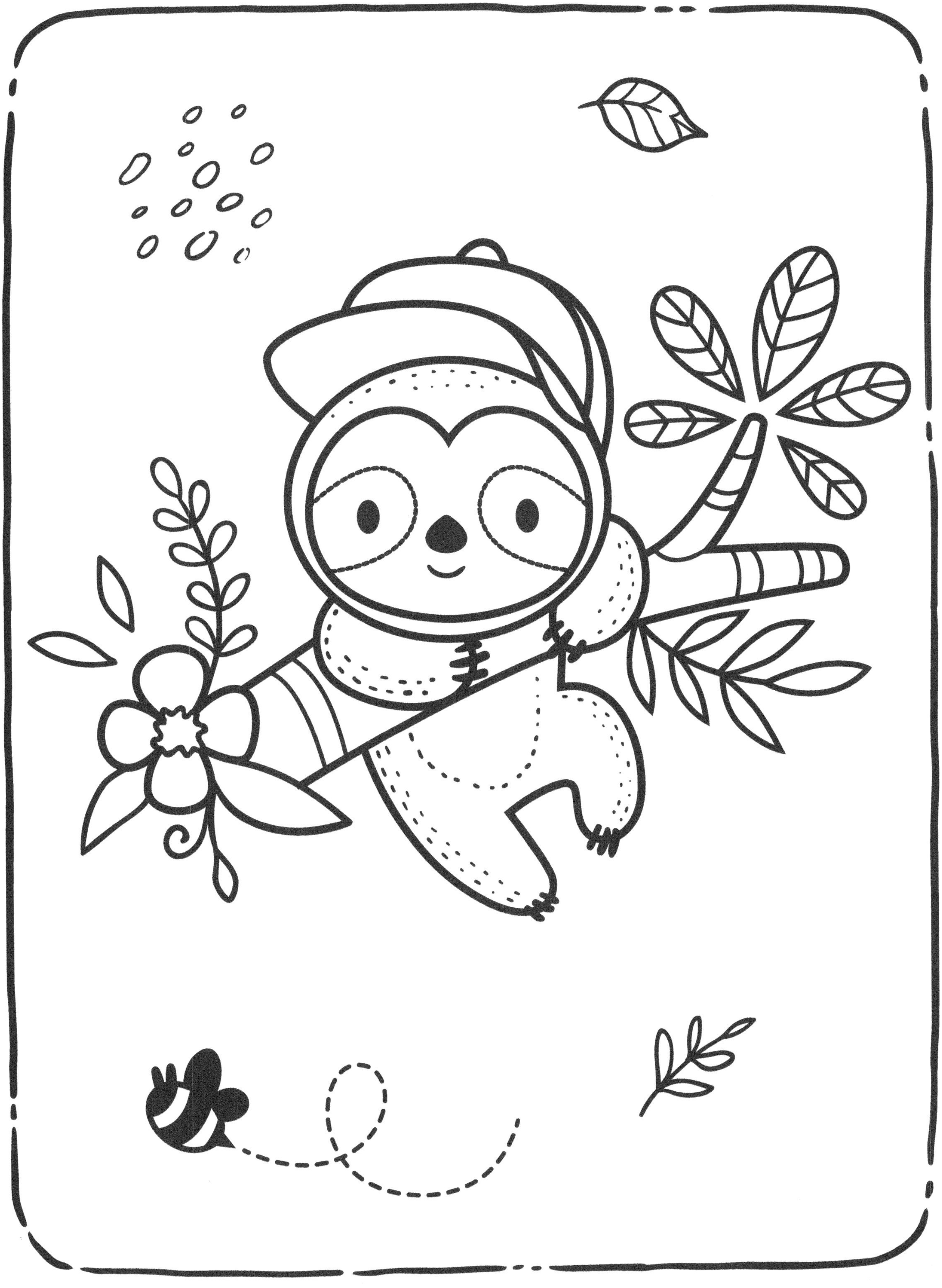

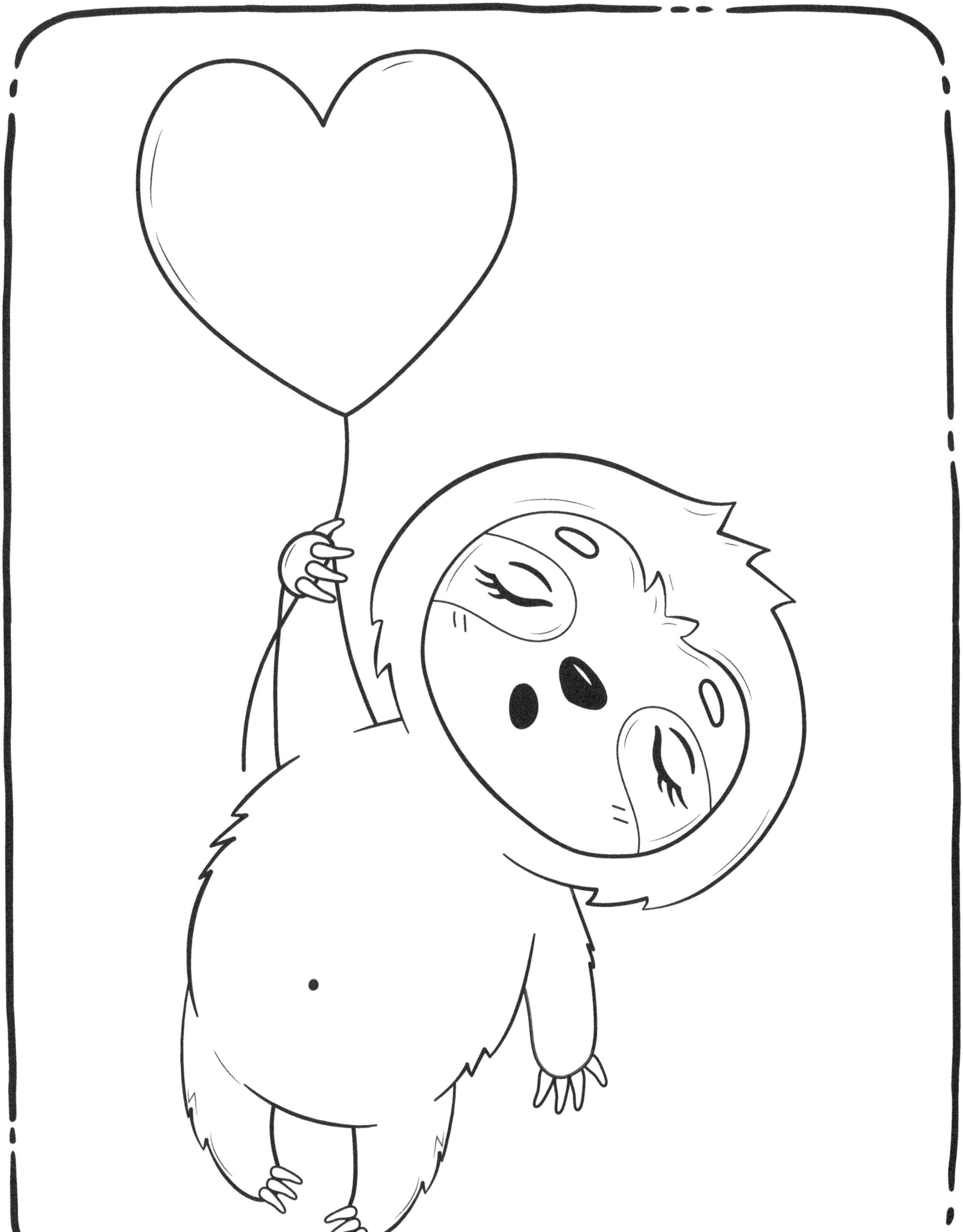

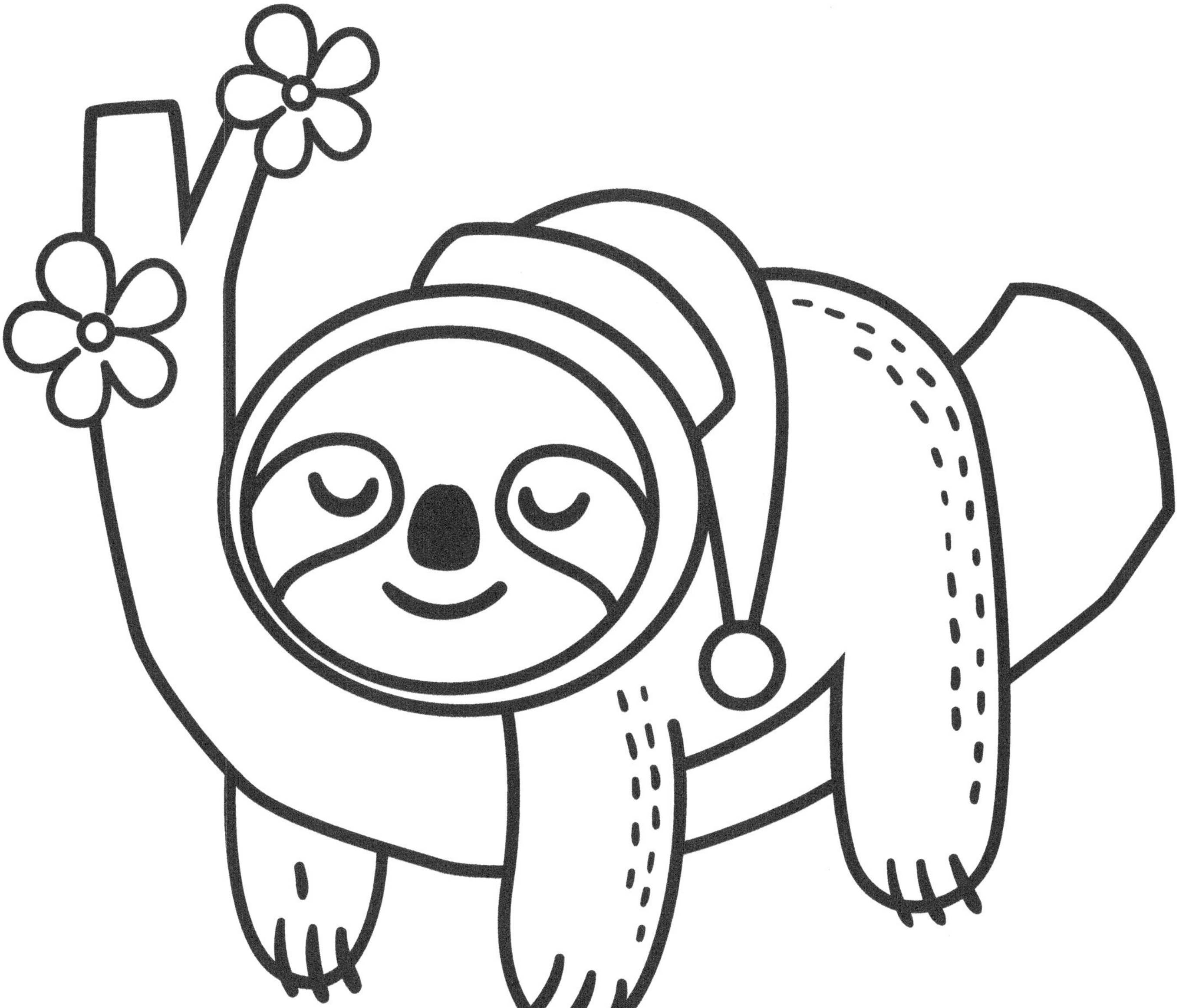

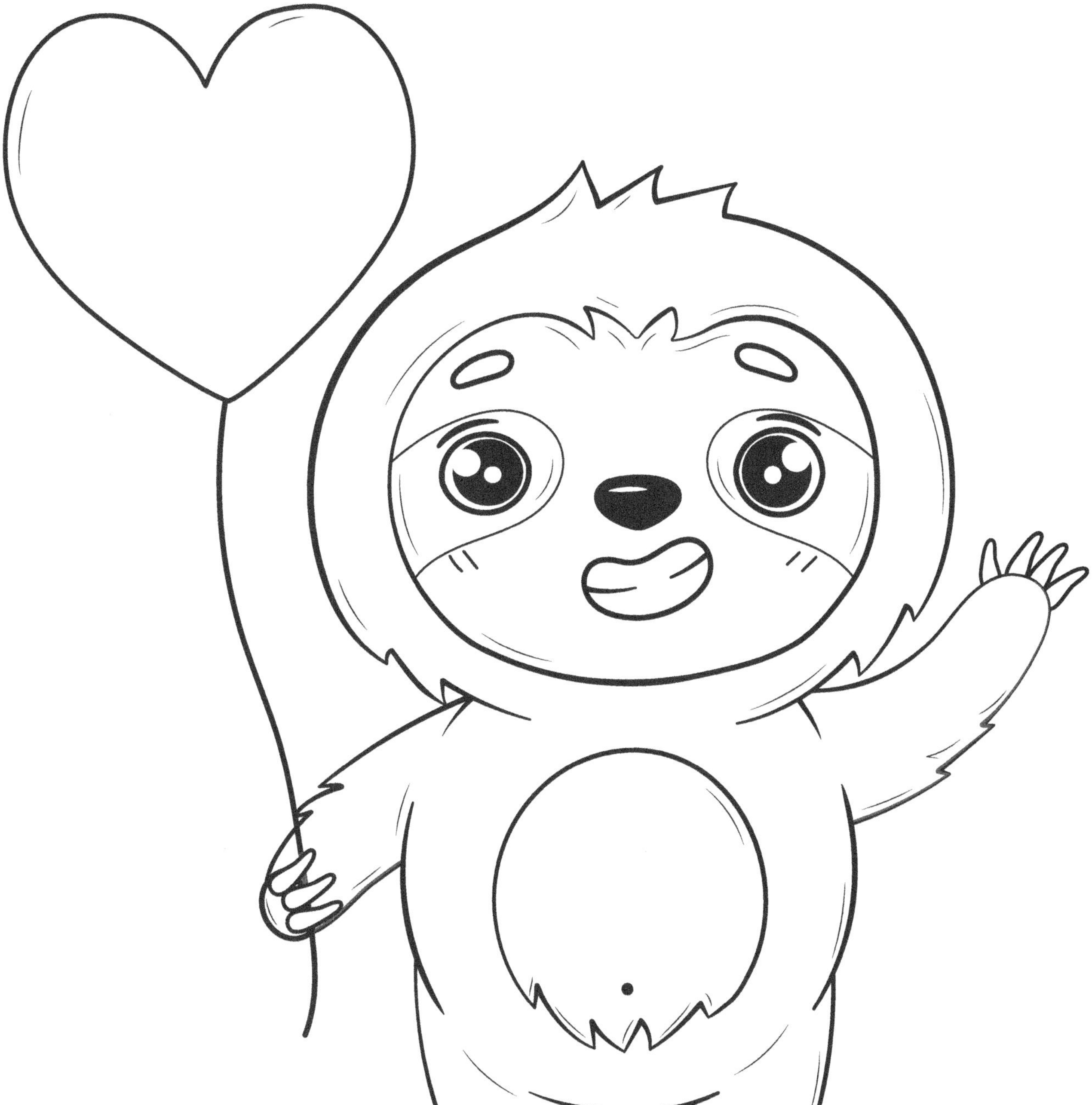

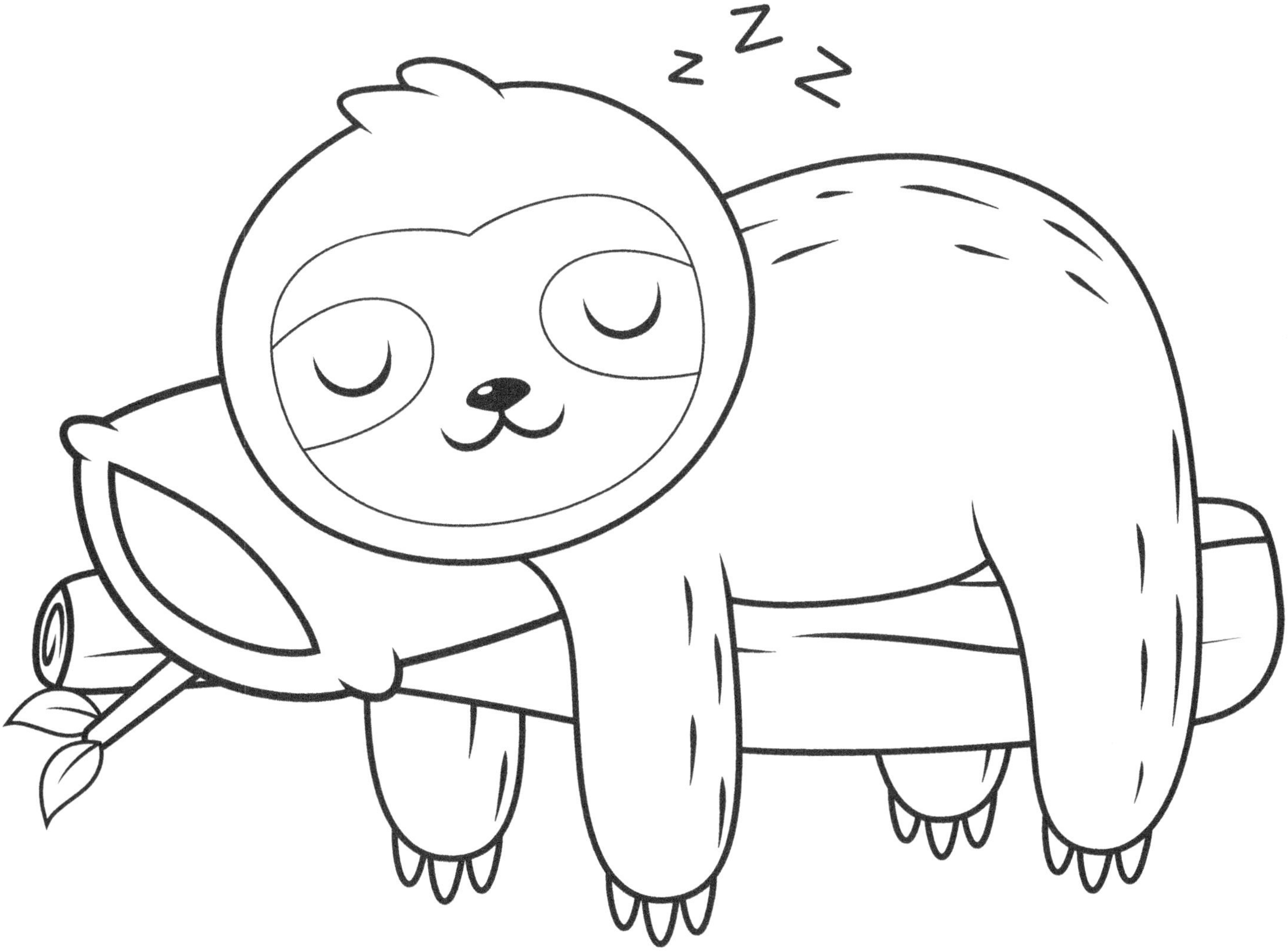
z Z Z

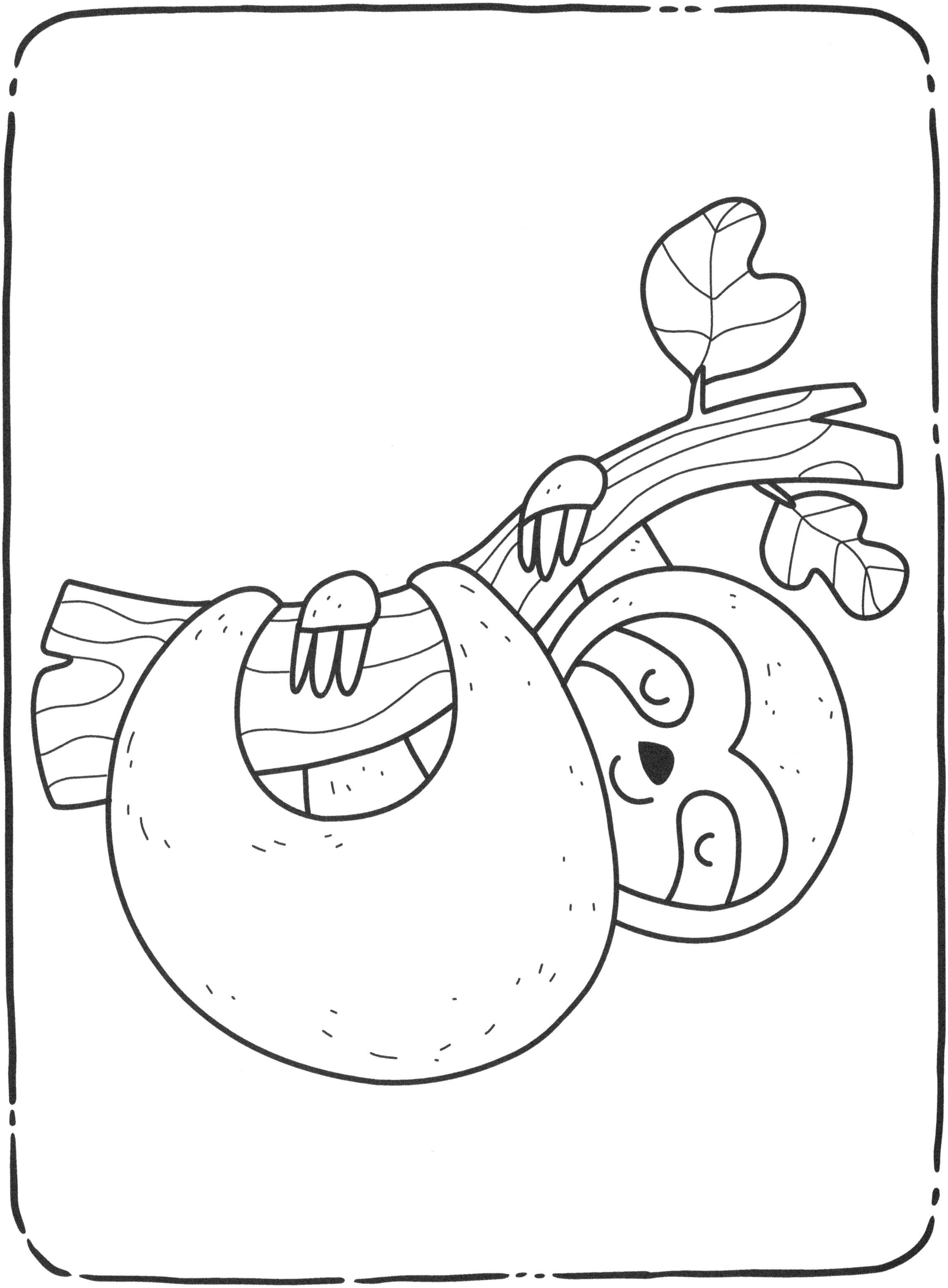

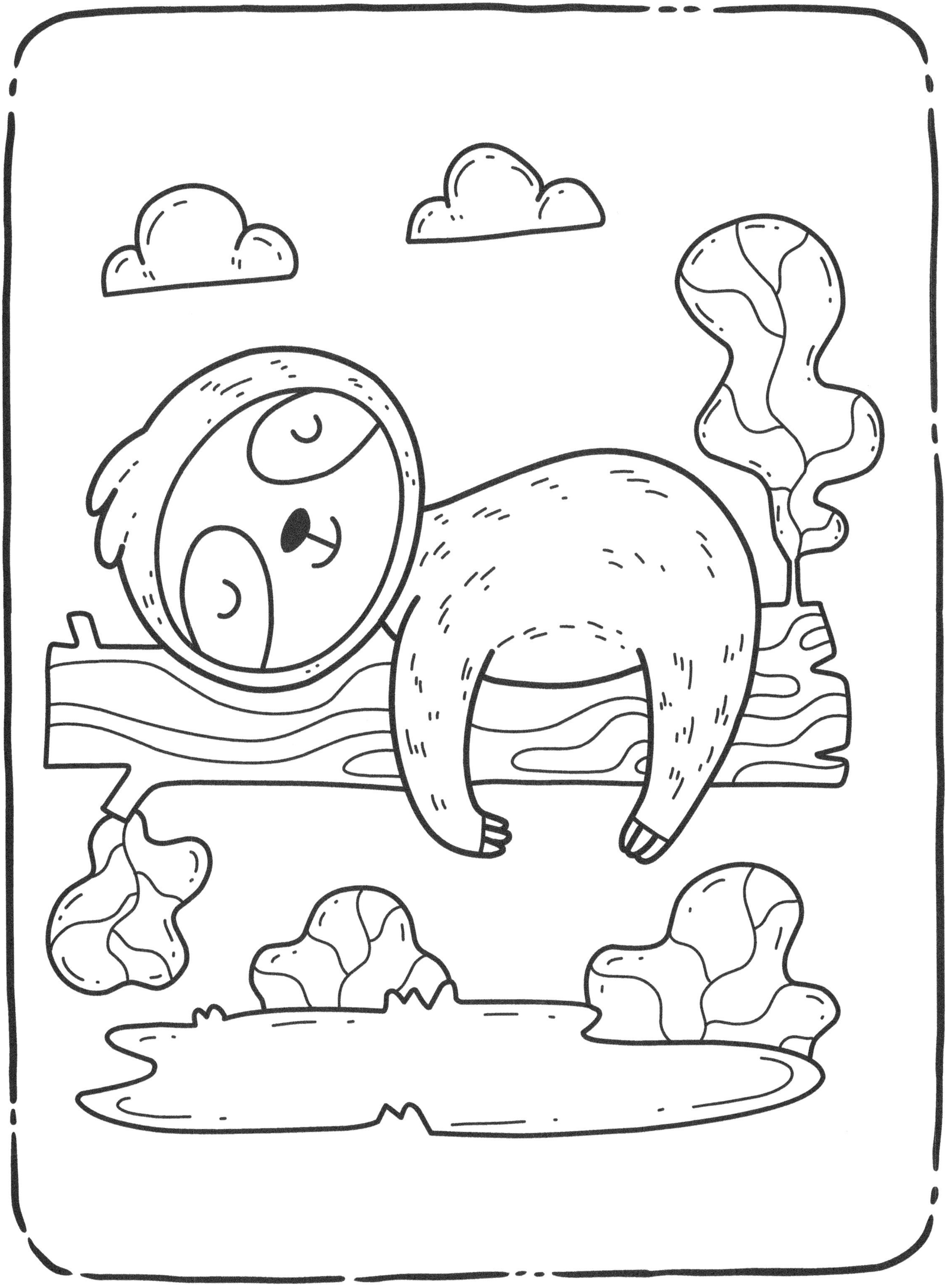

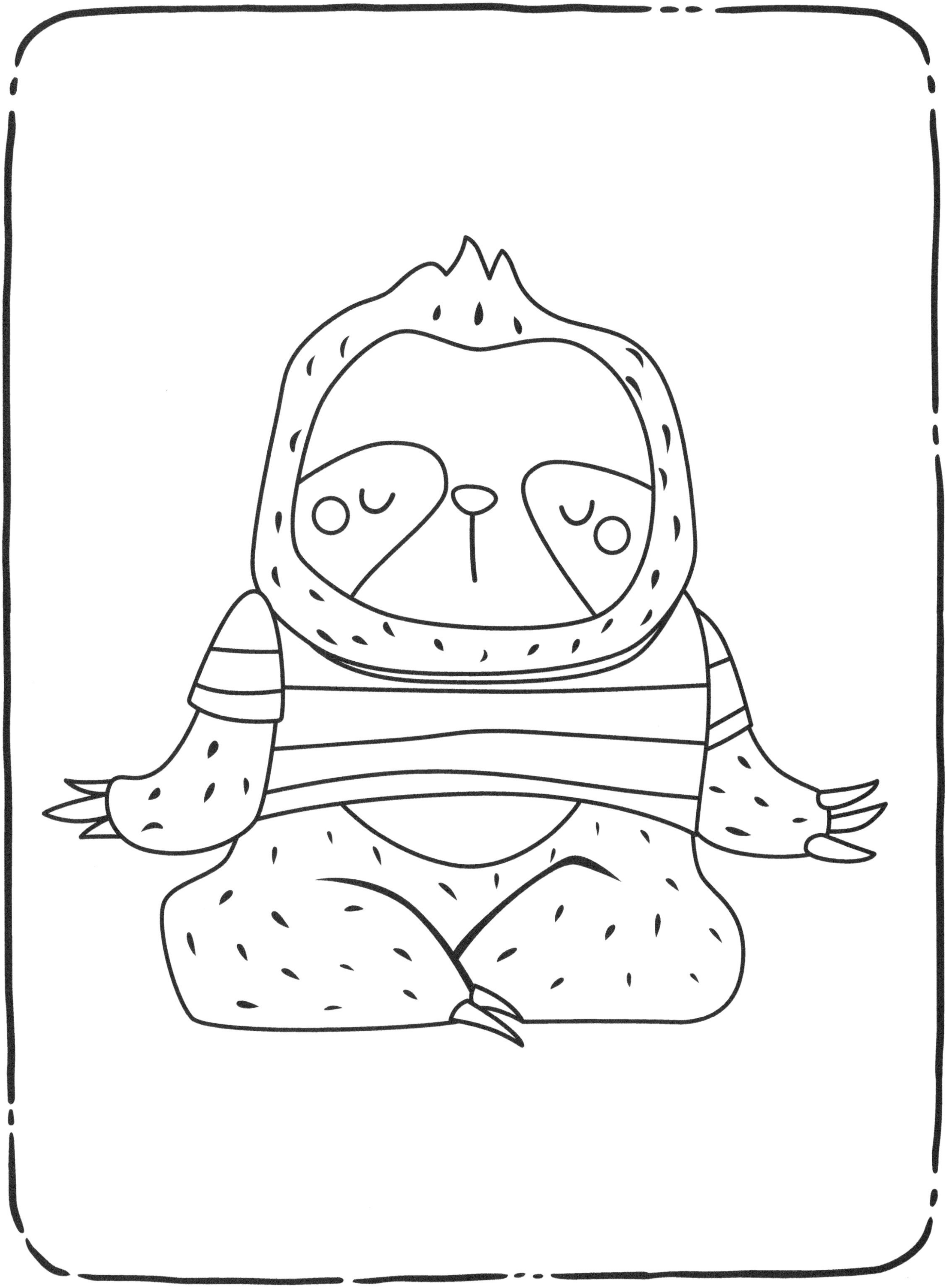

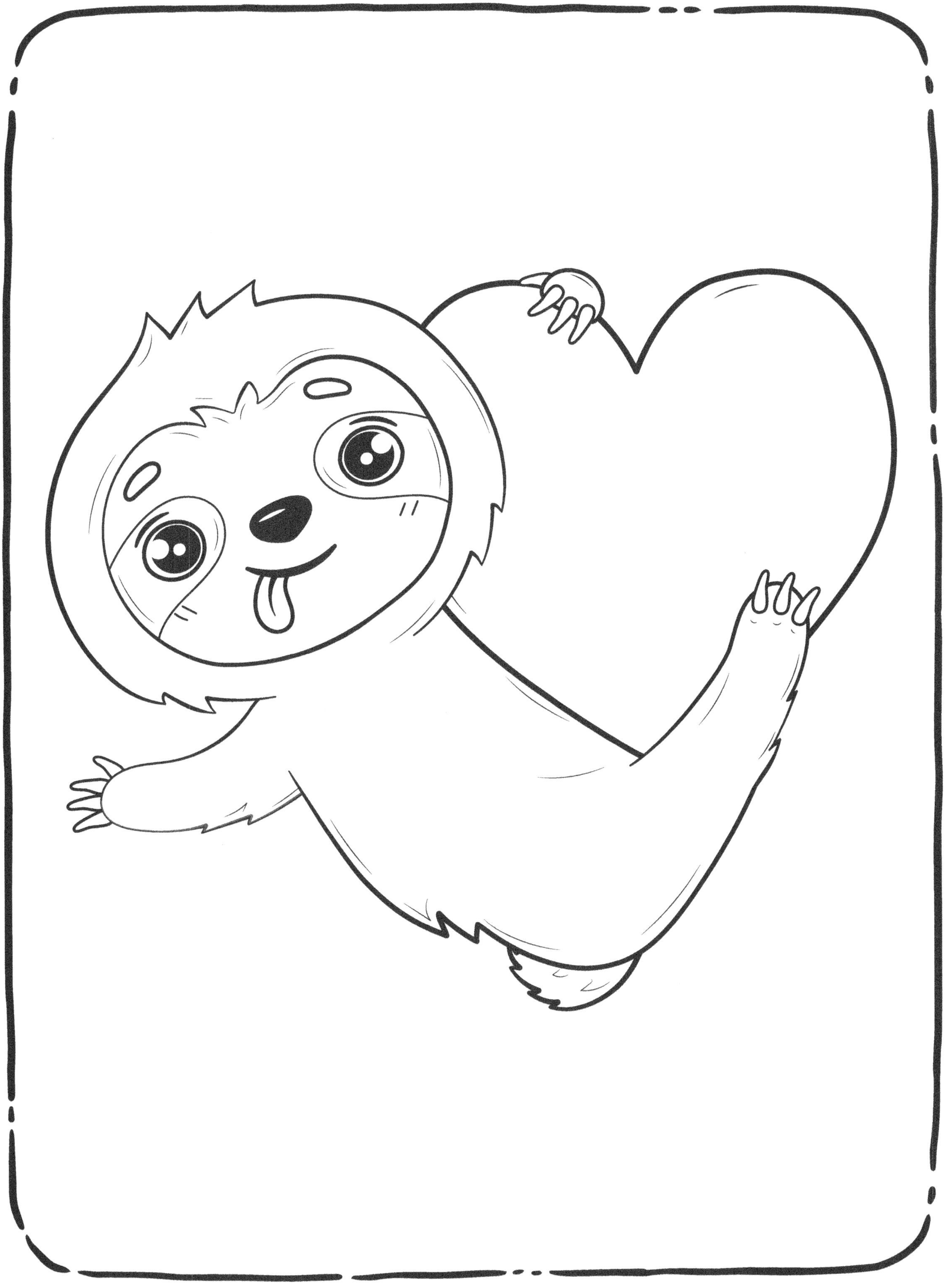

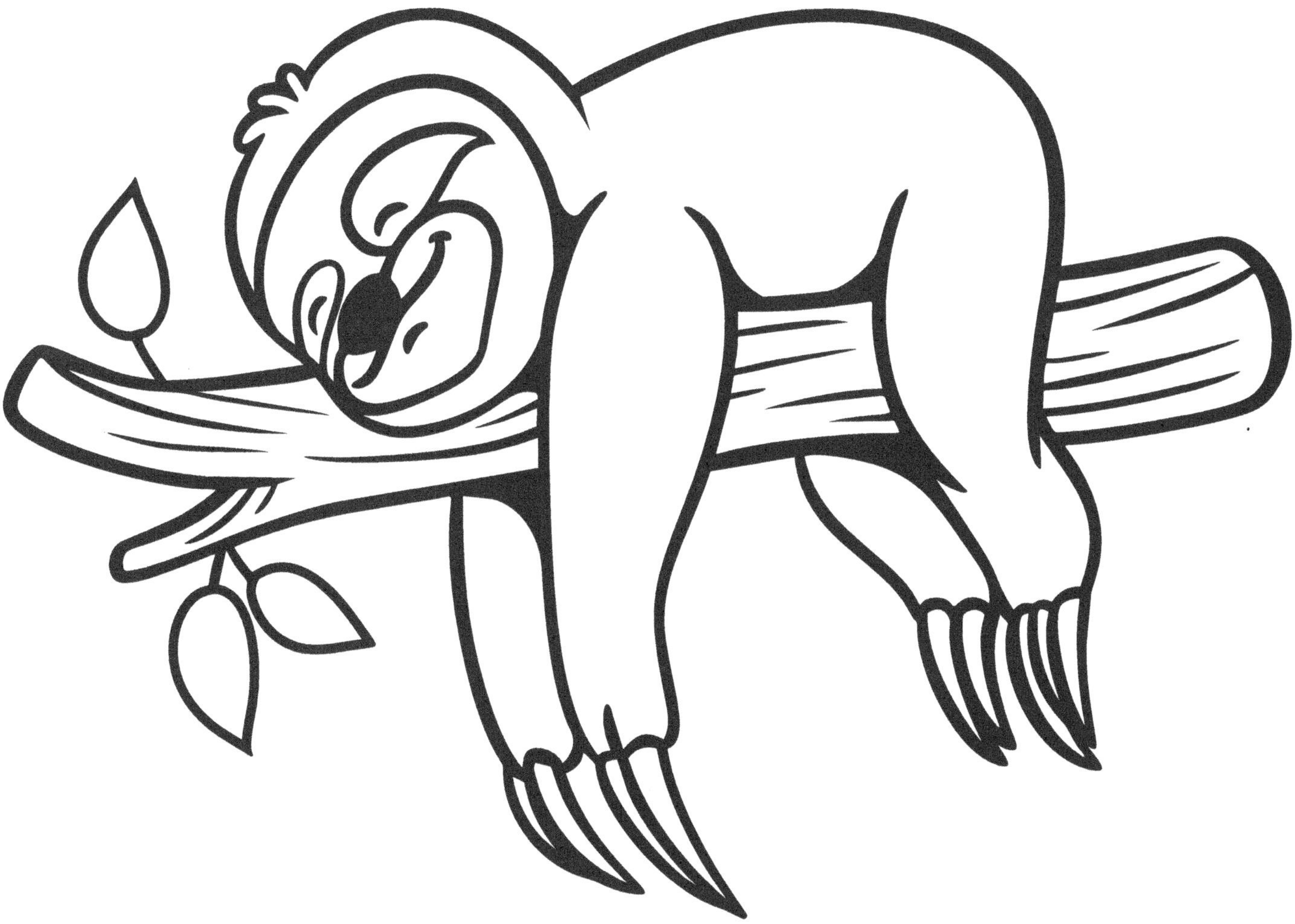

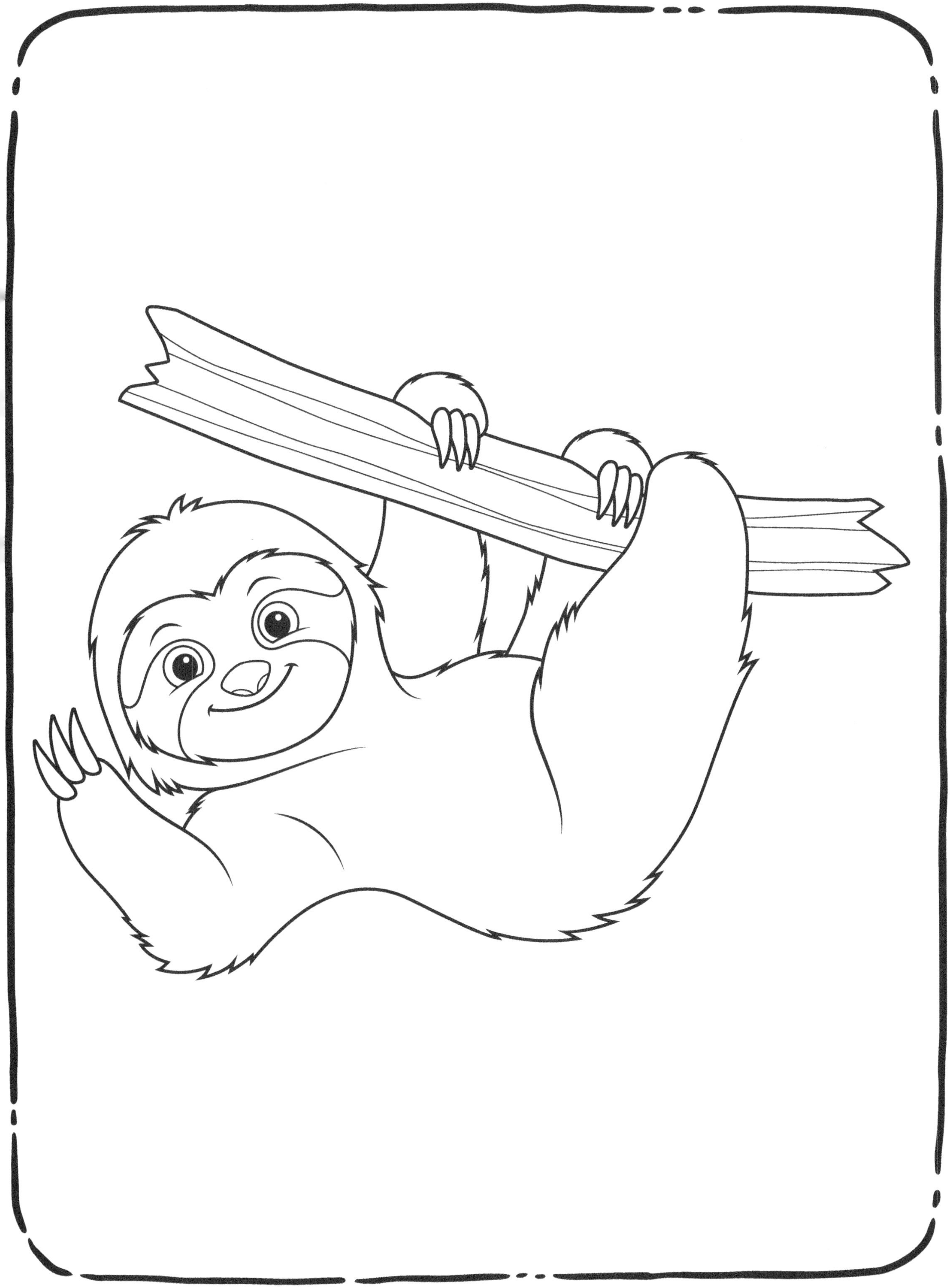

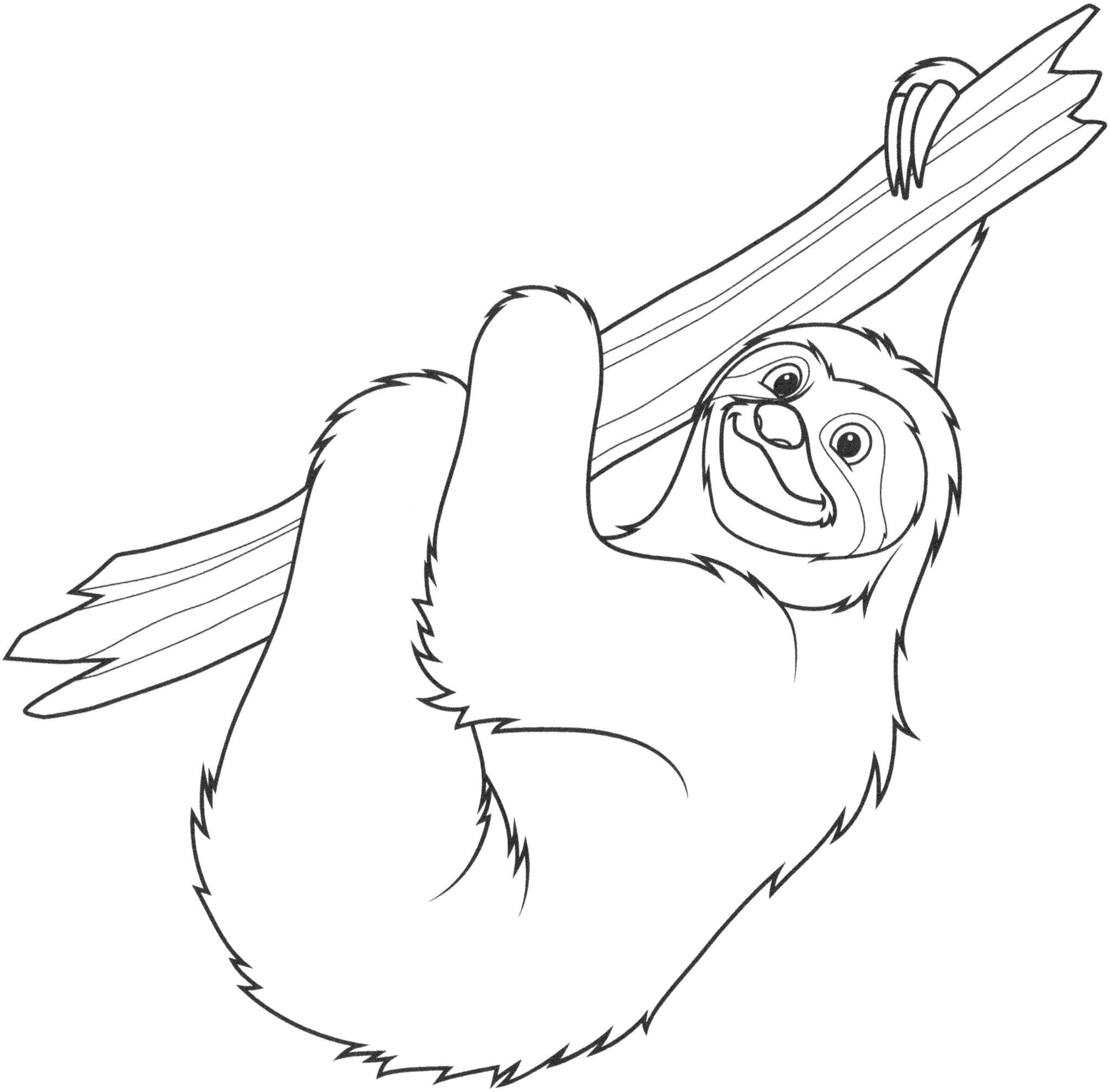

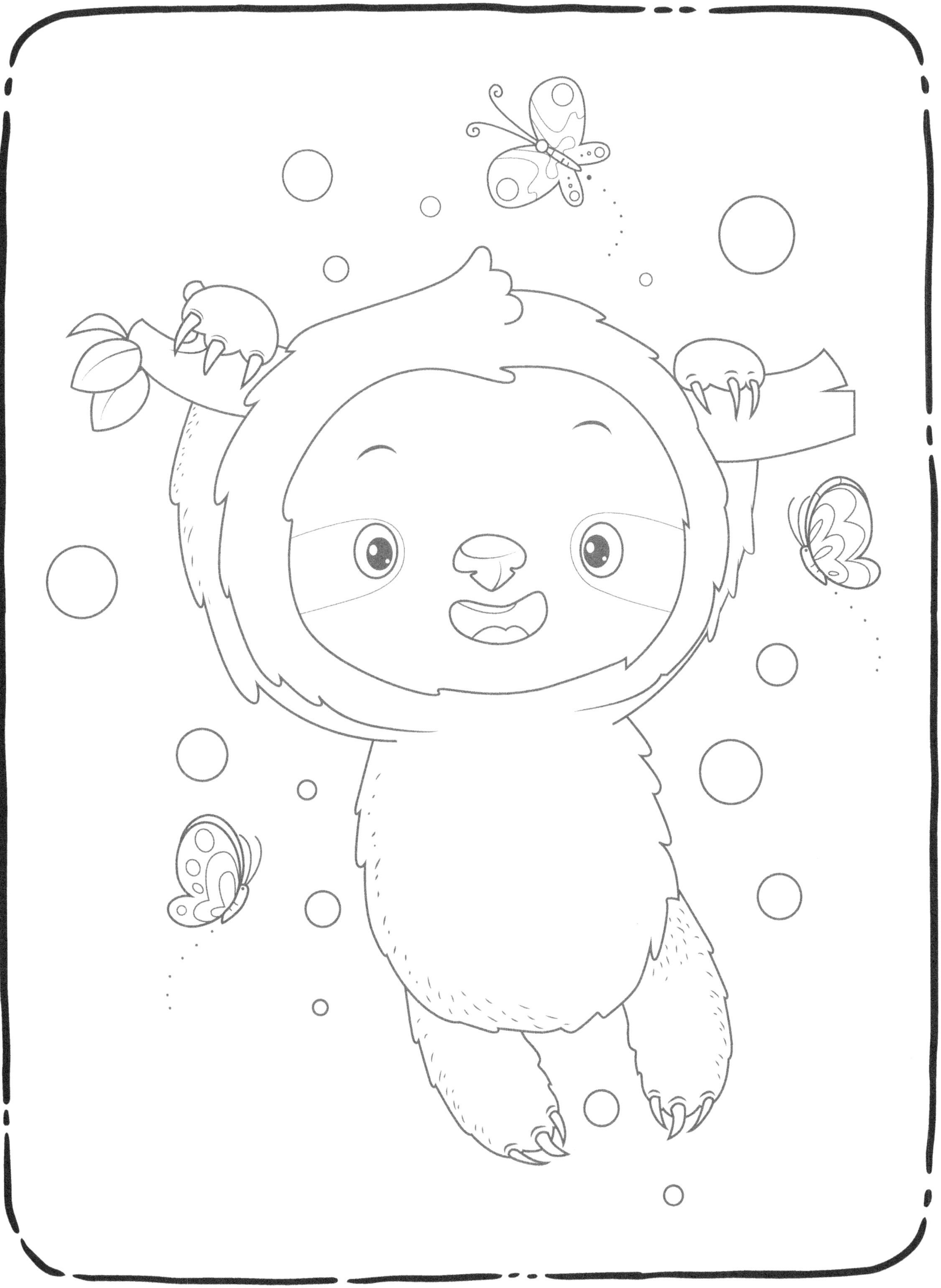

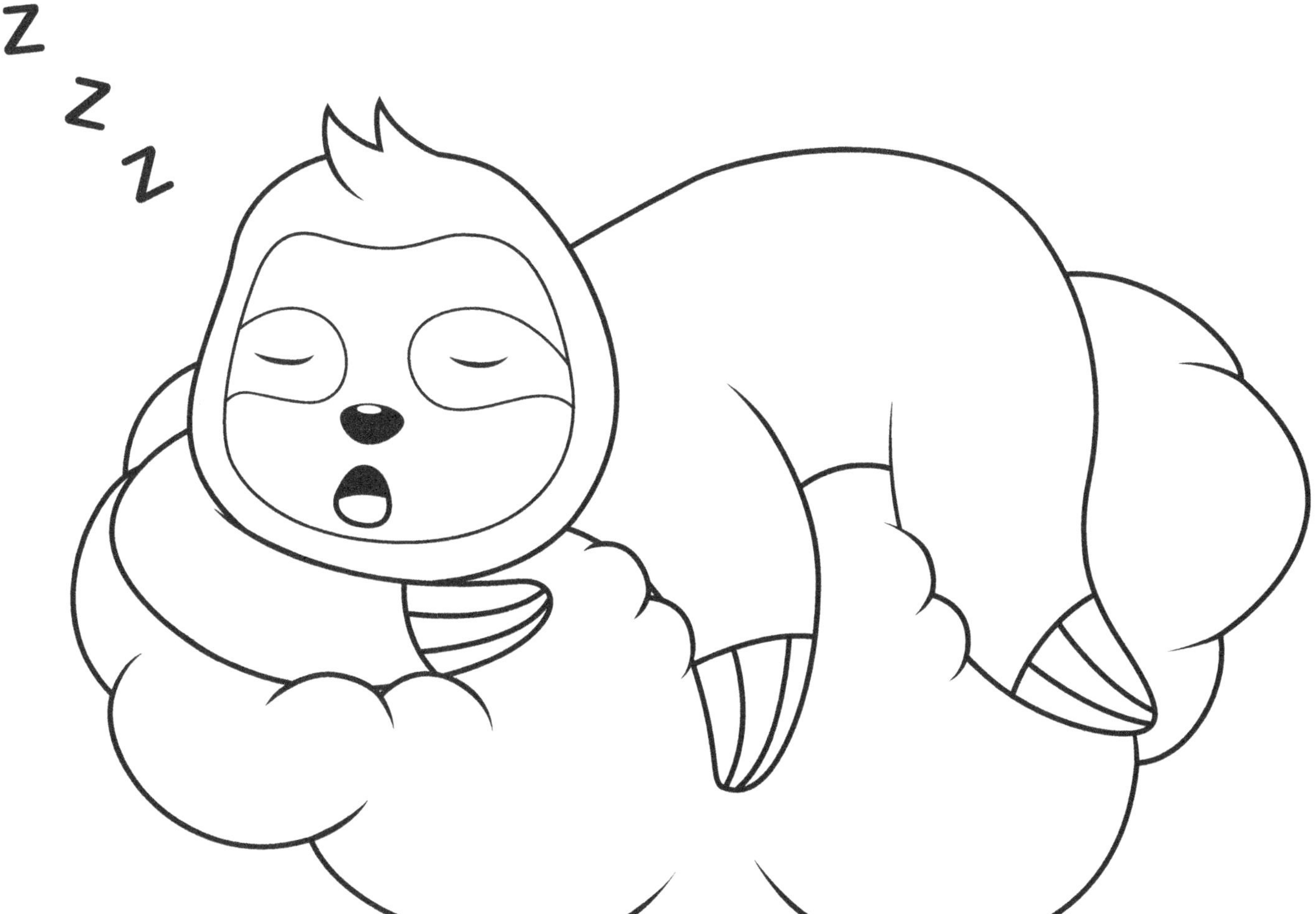
Z Z Z

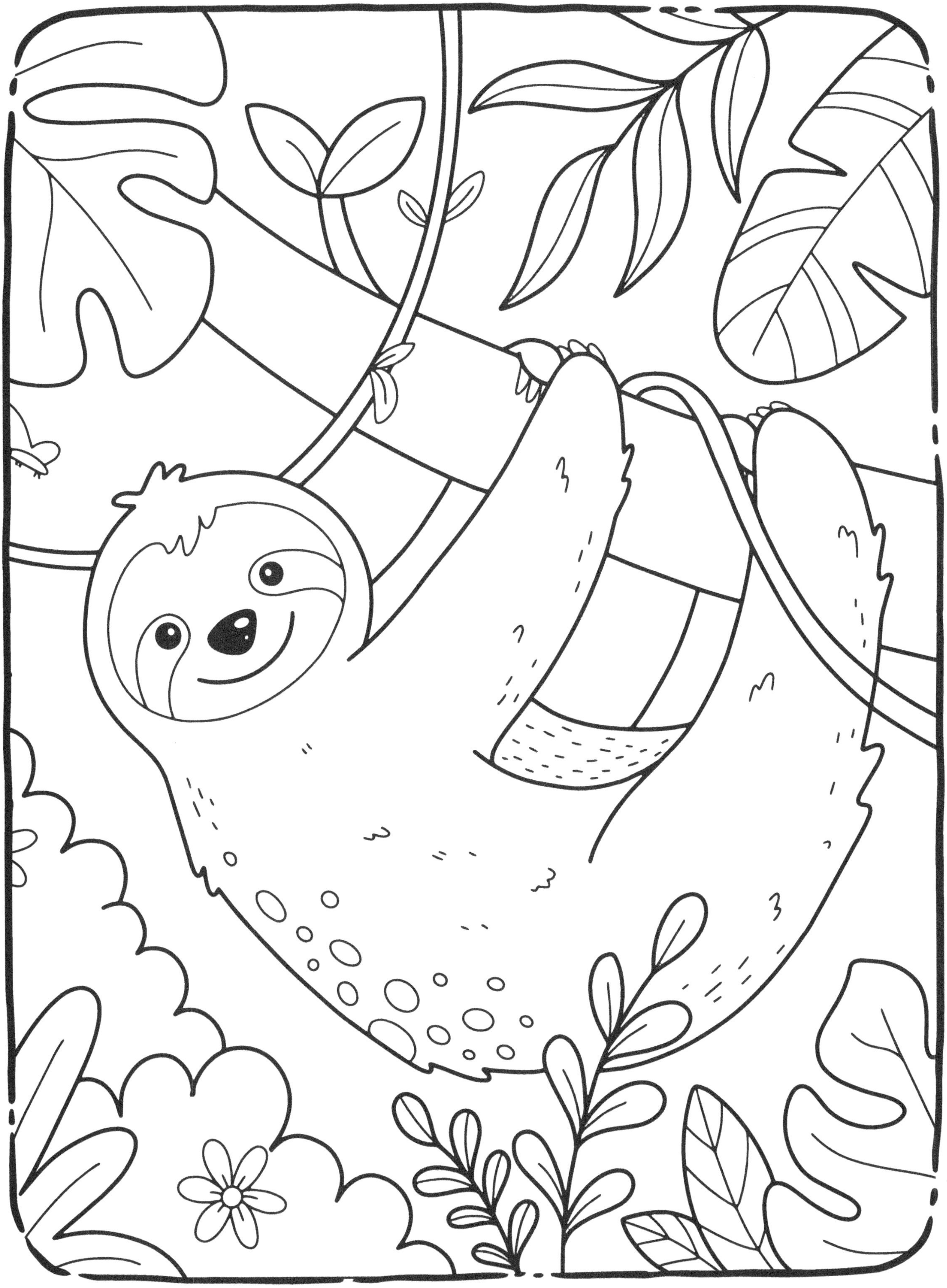

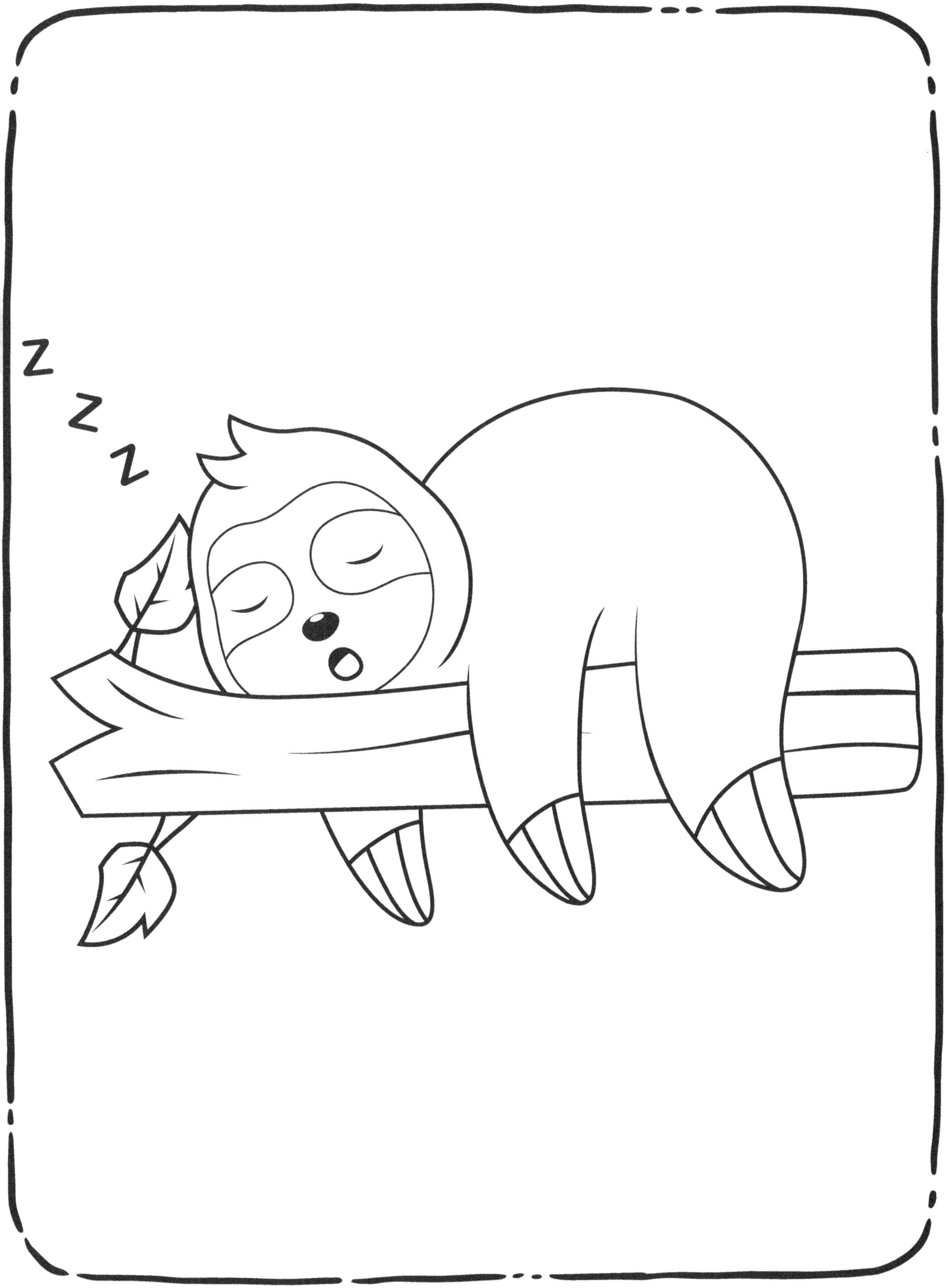
Z Z Z

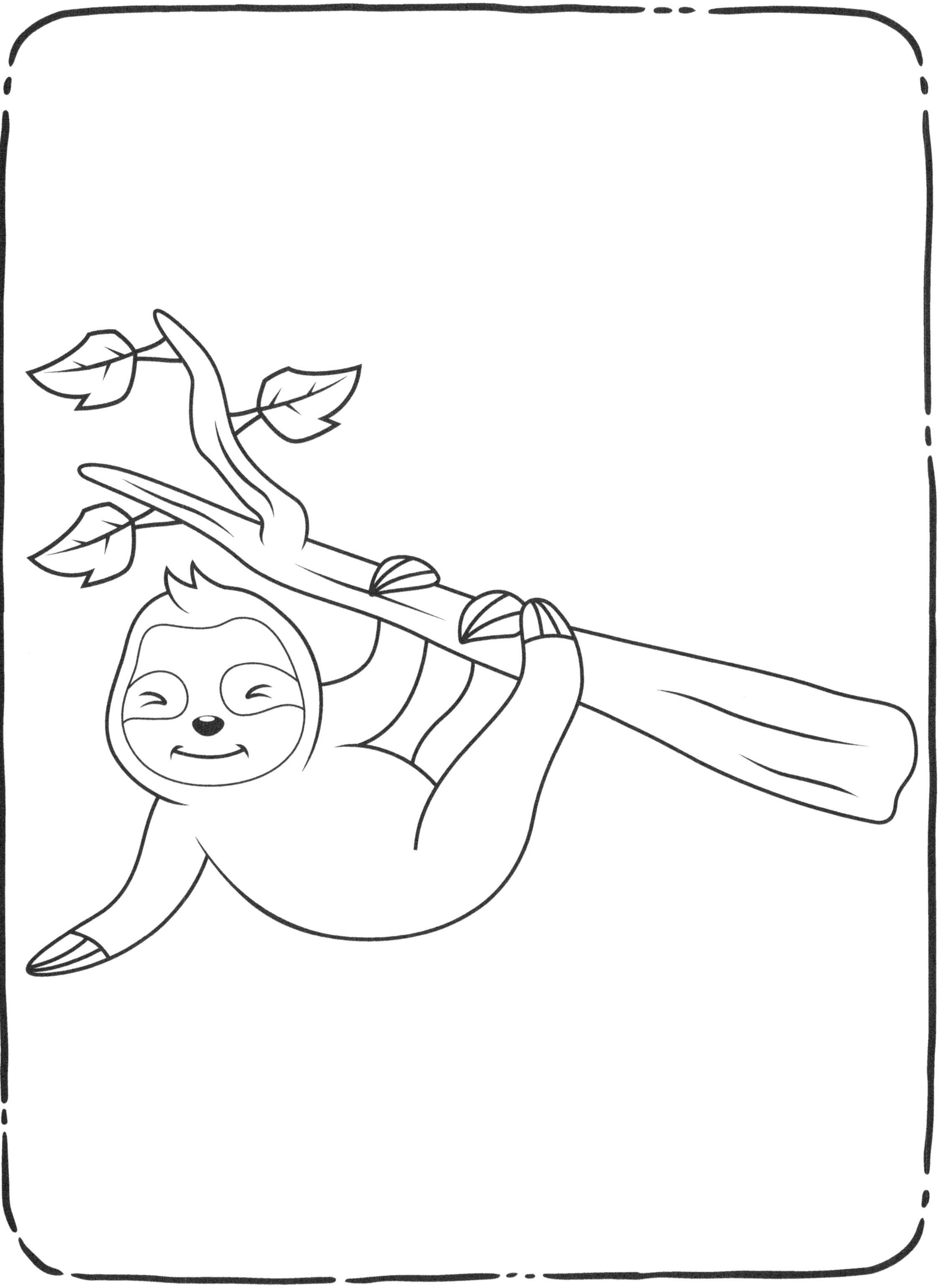

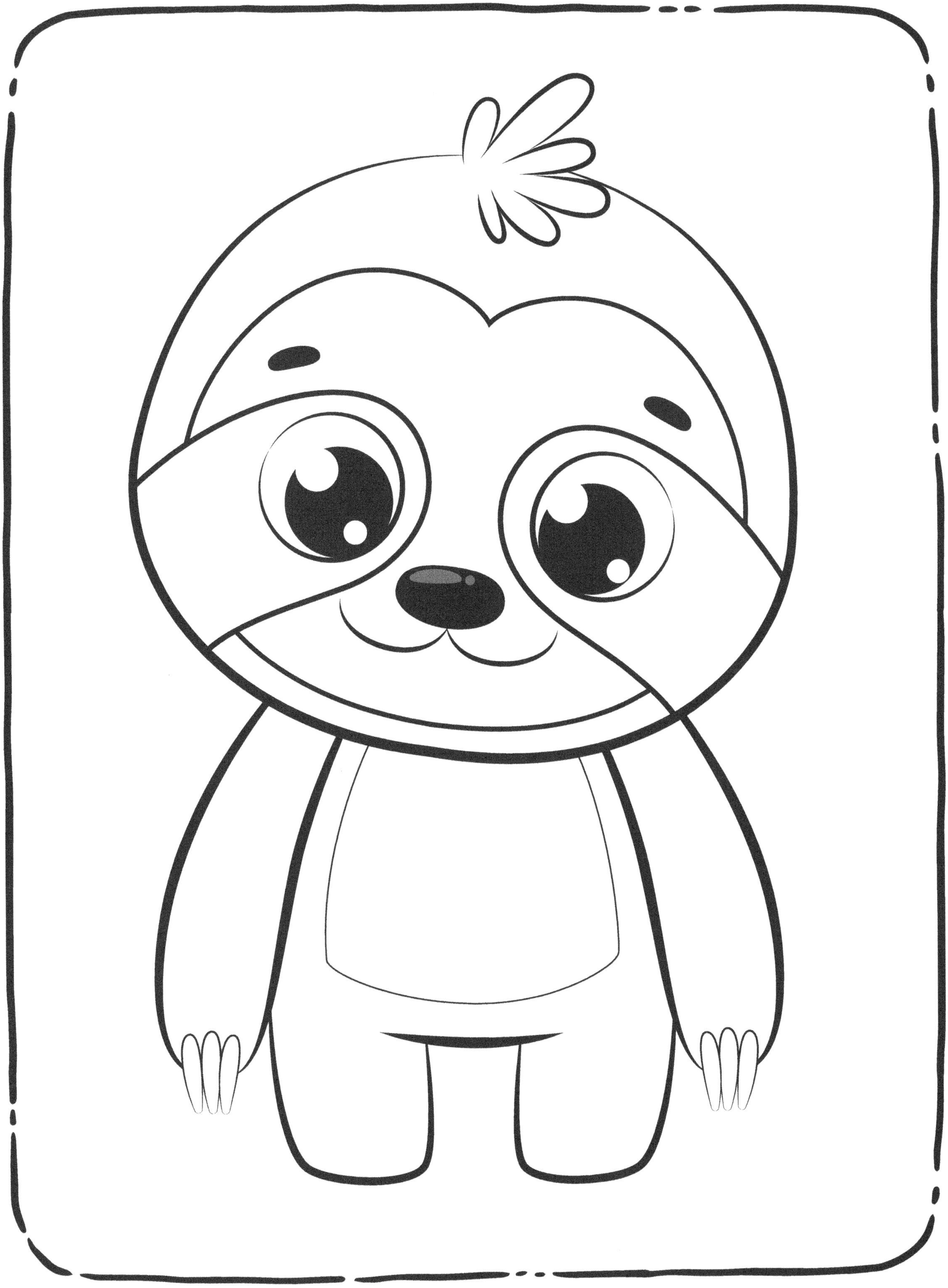

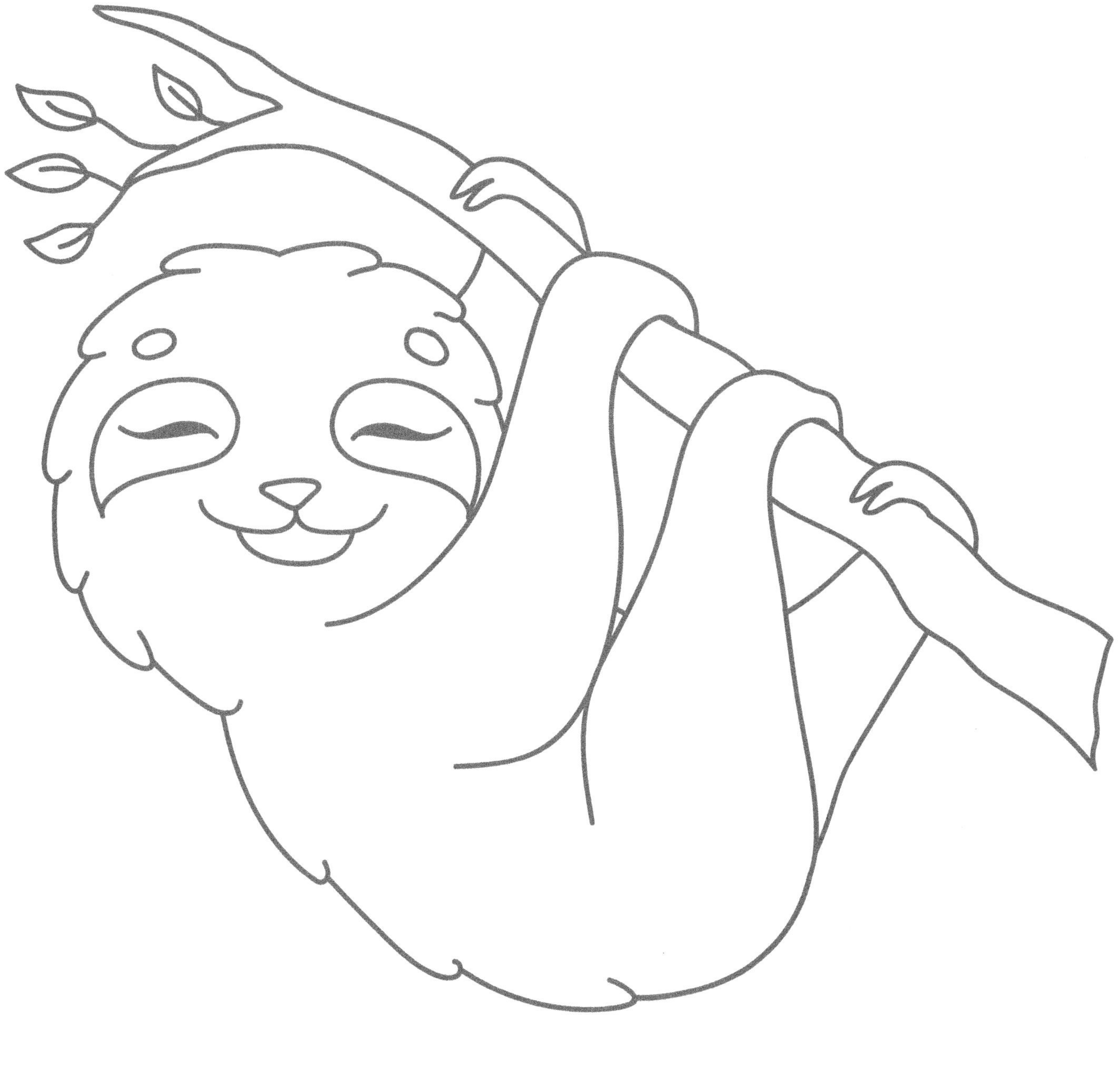

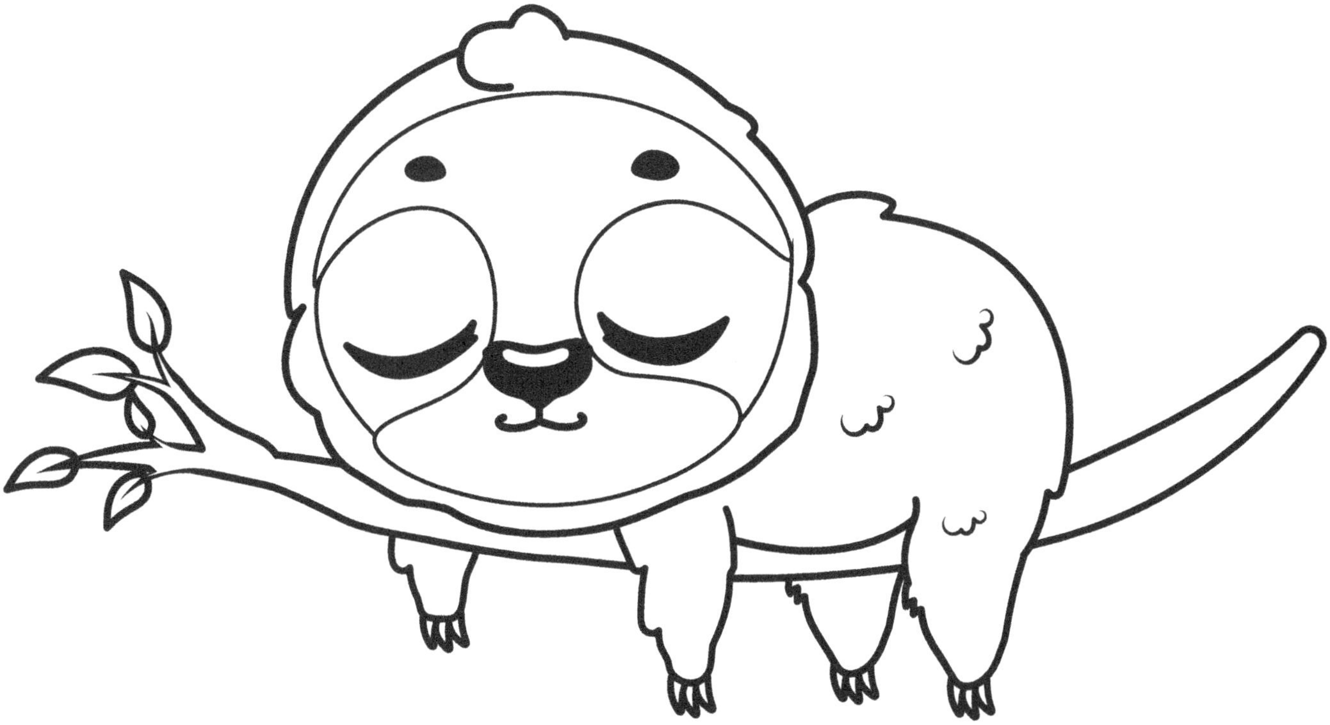

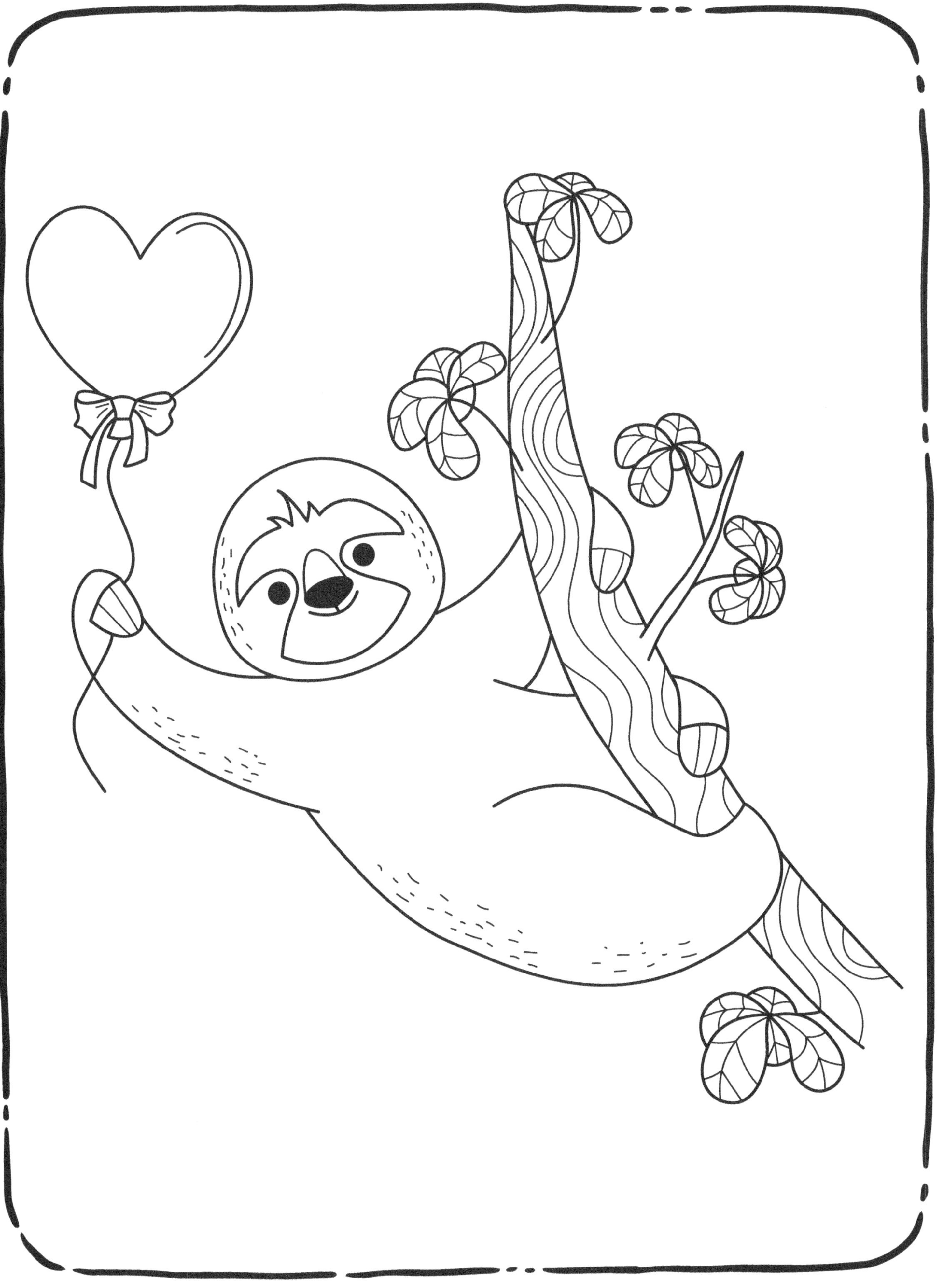

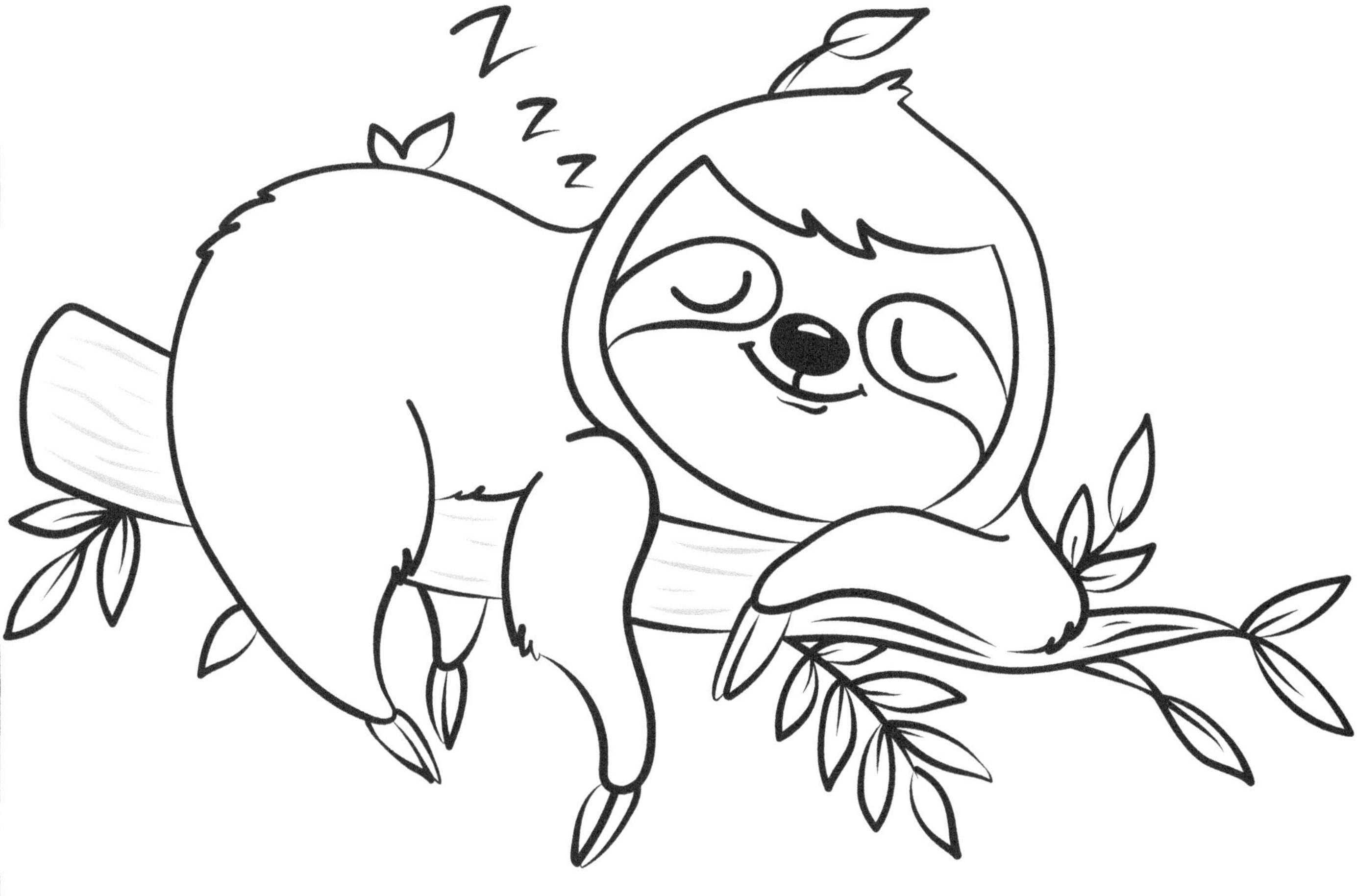

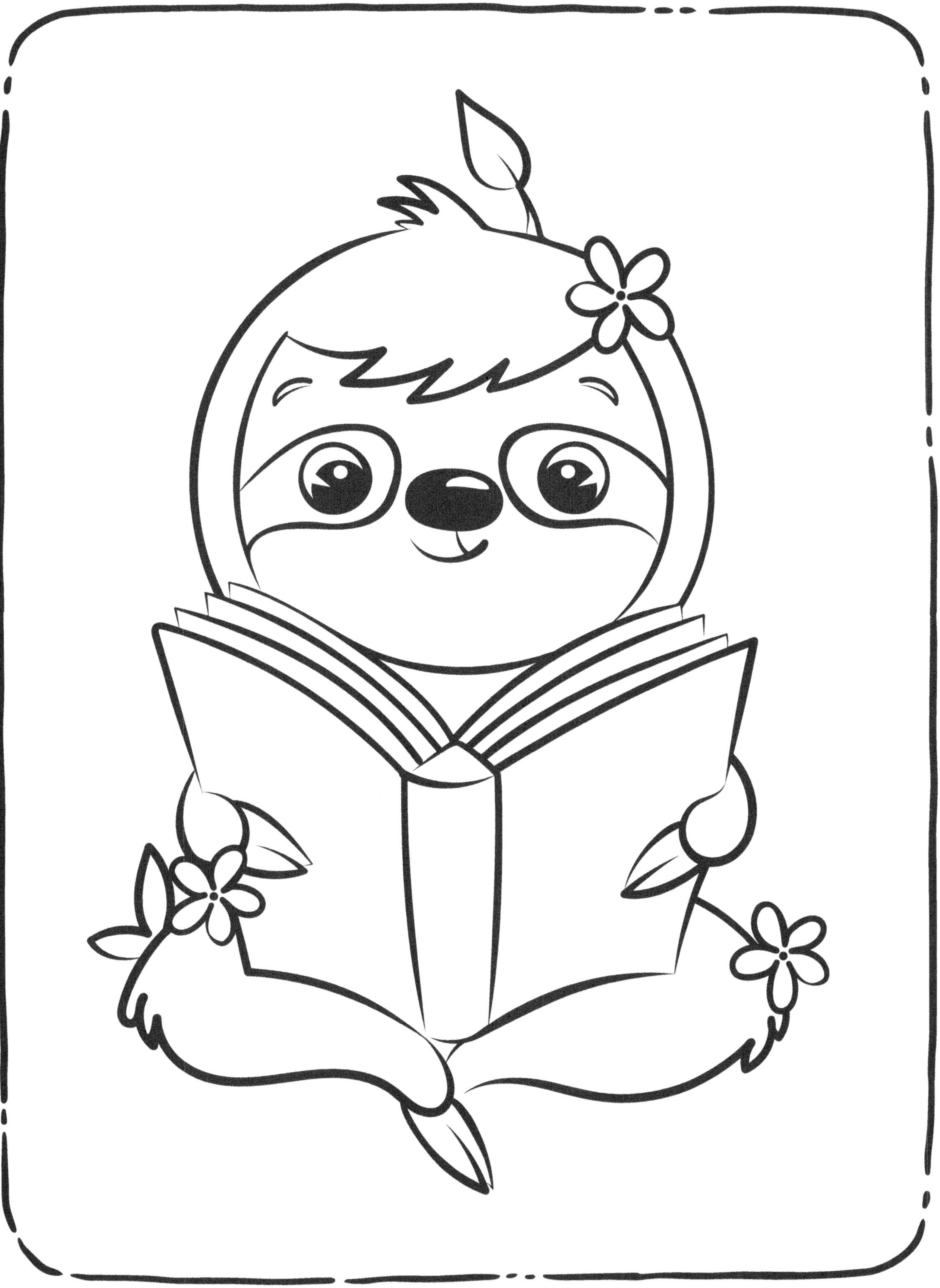

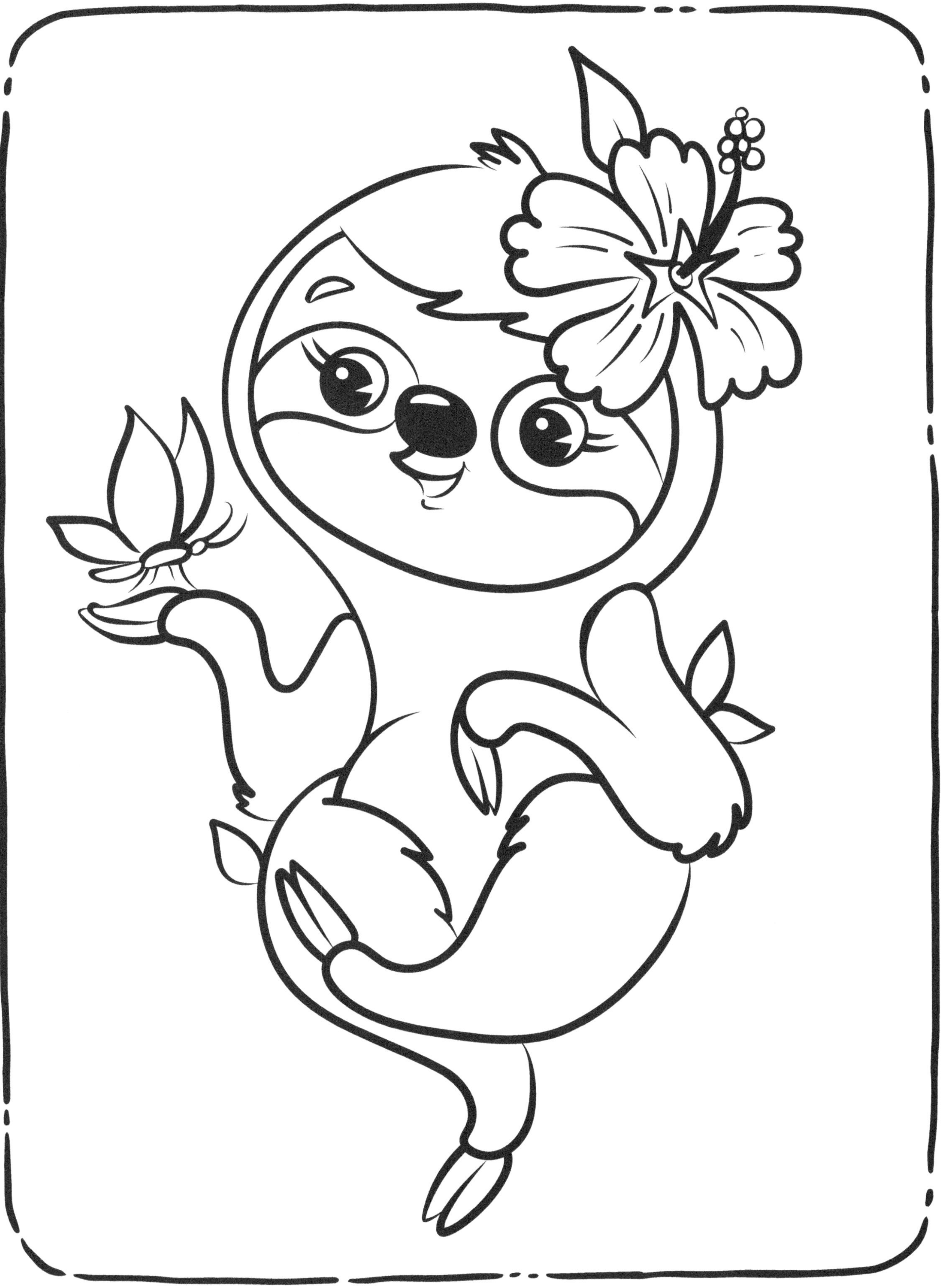

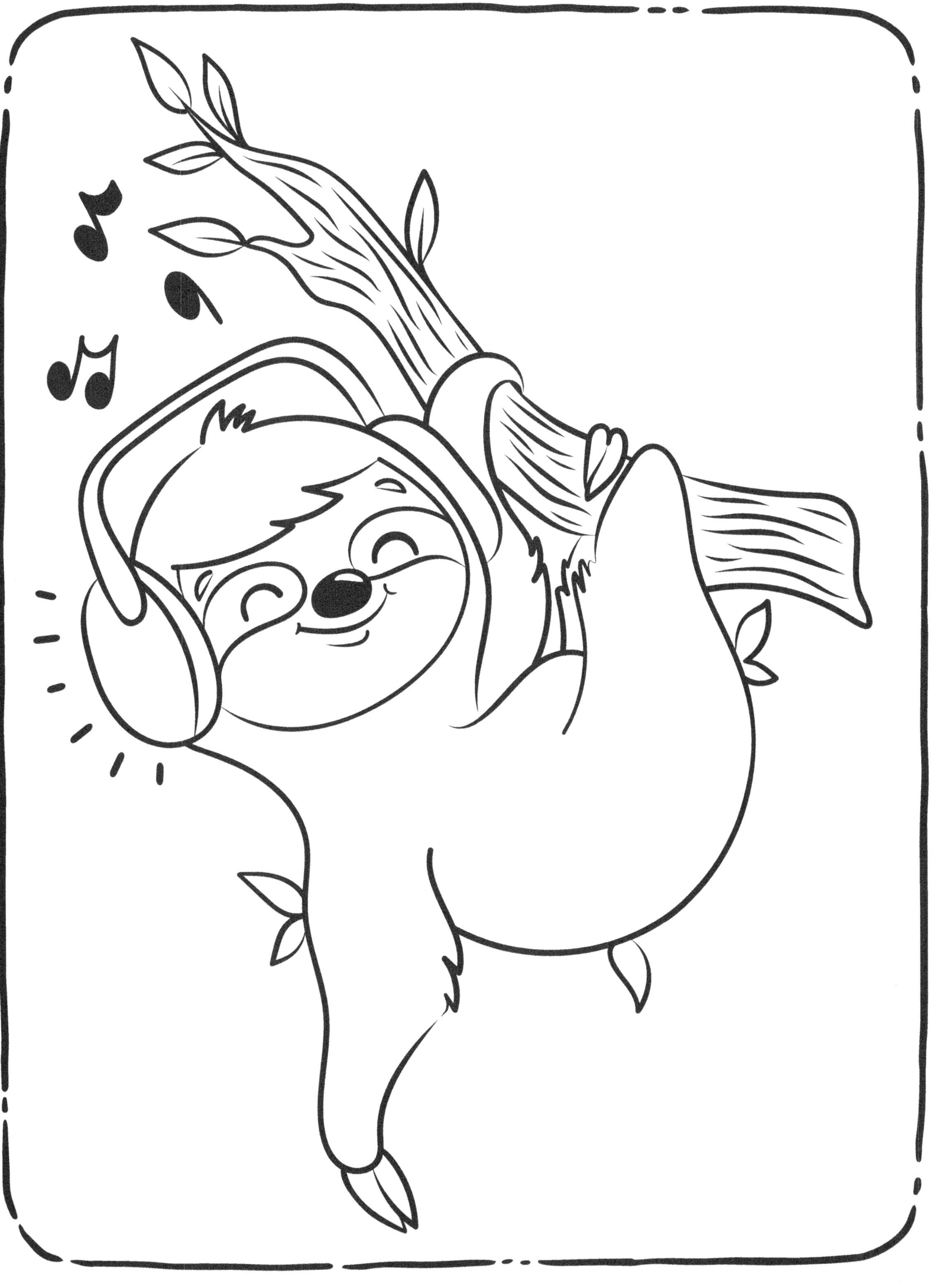

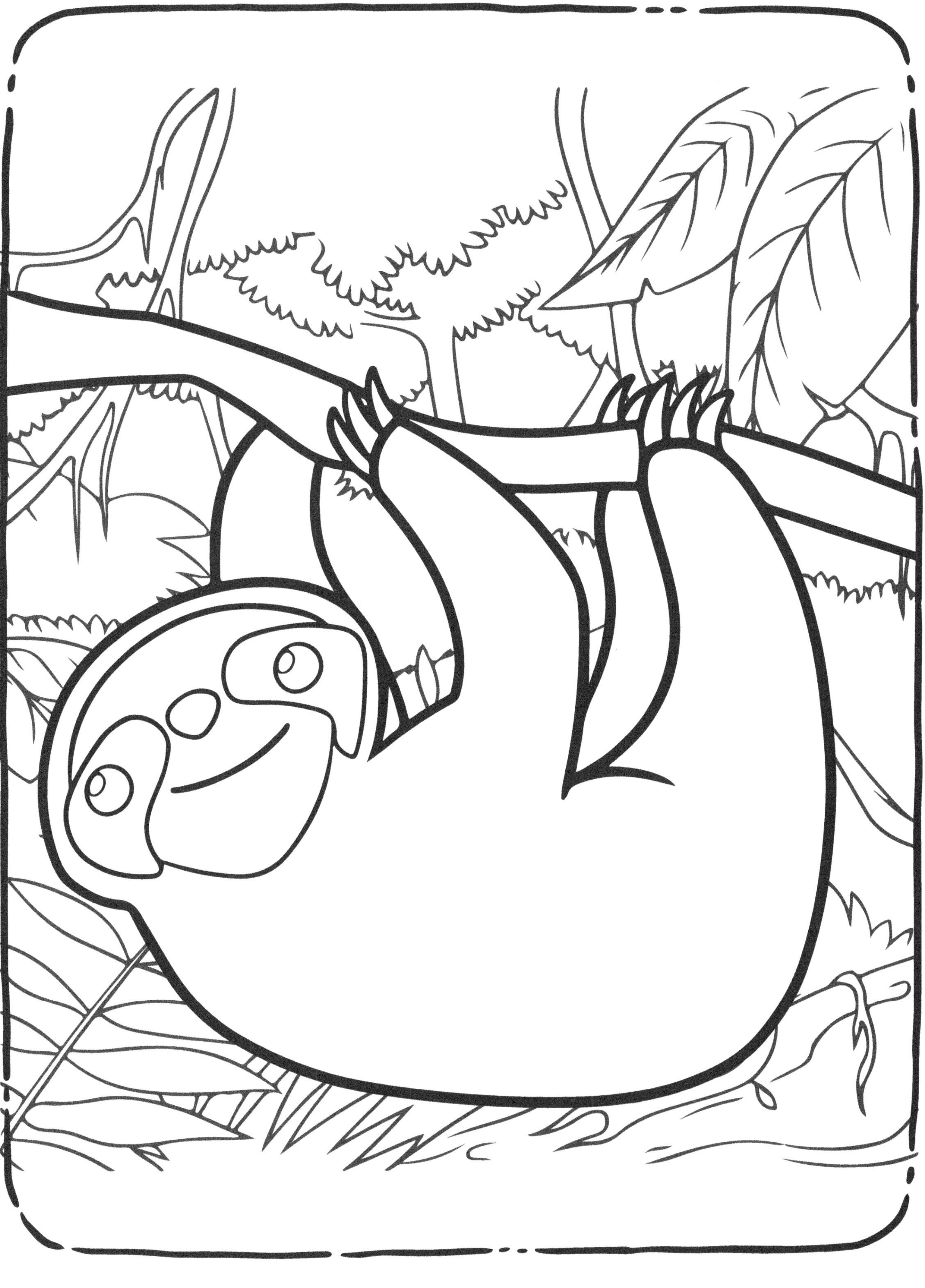

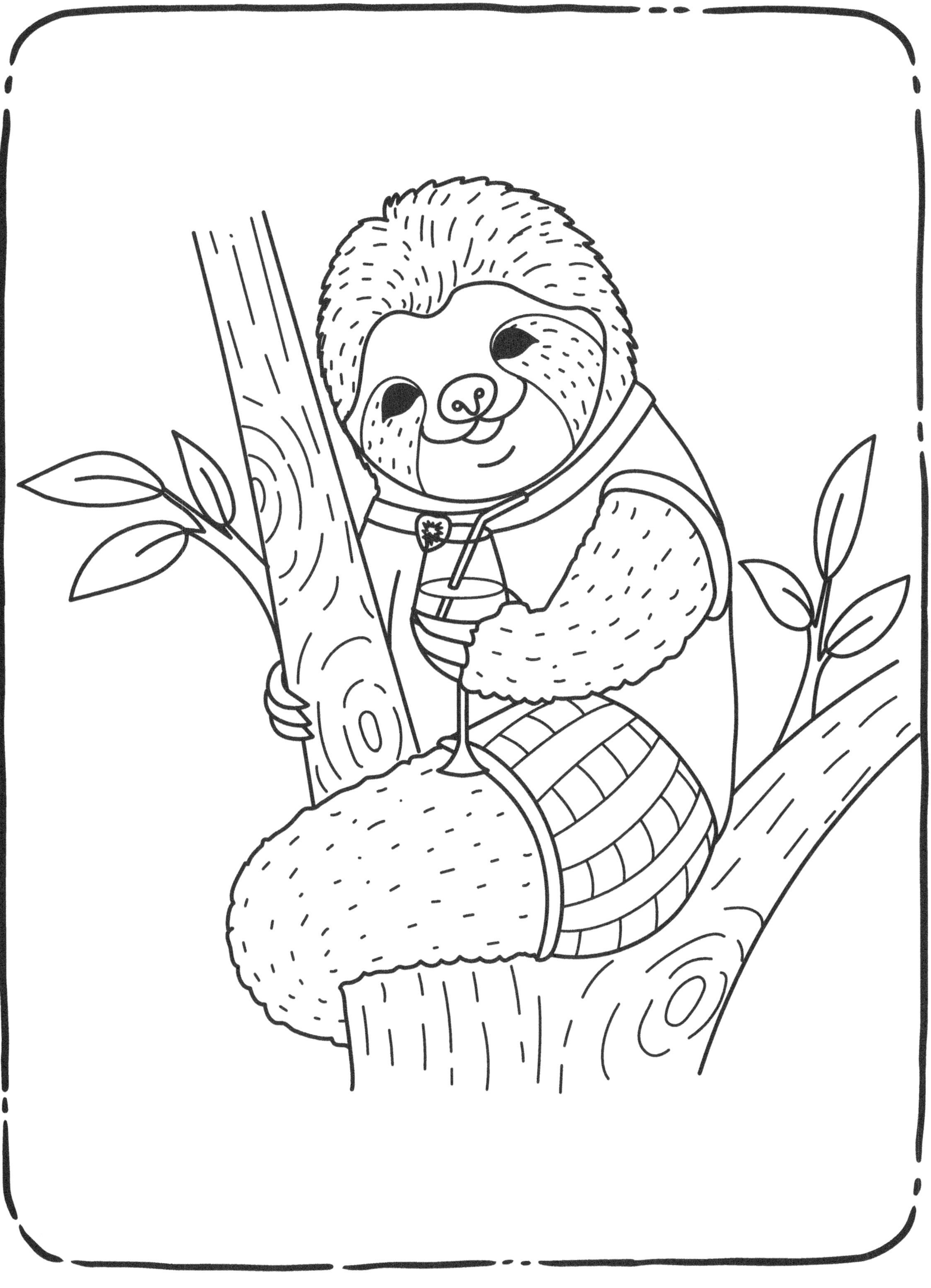

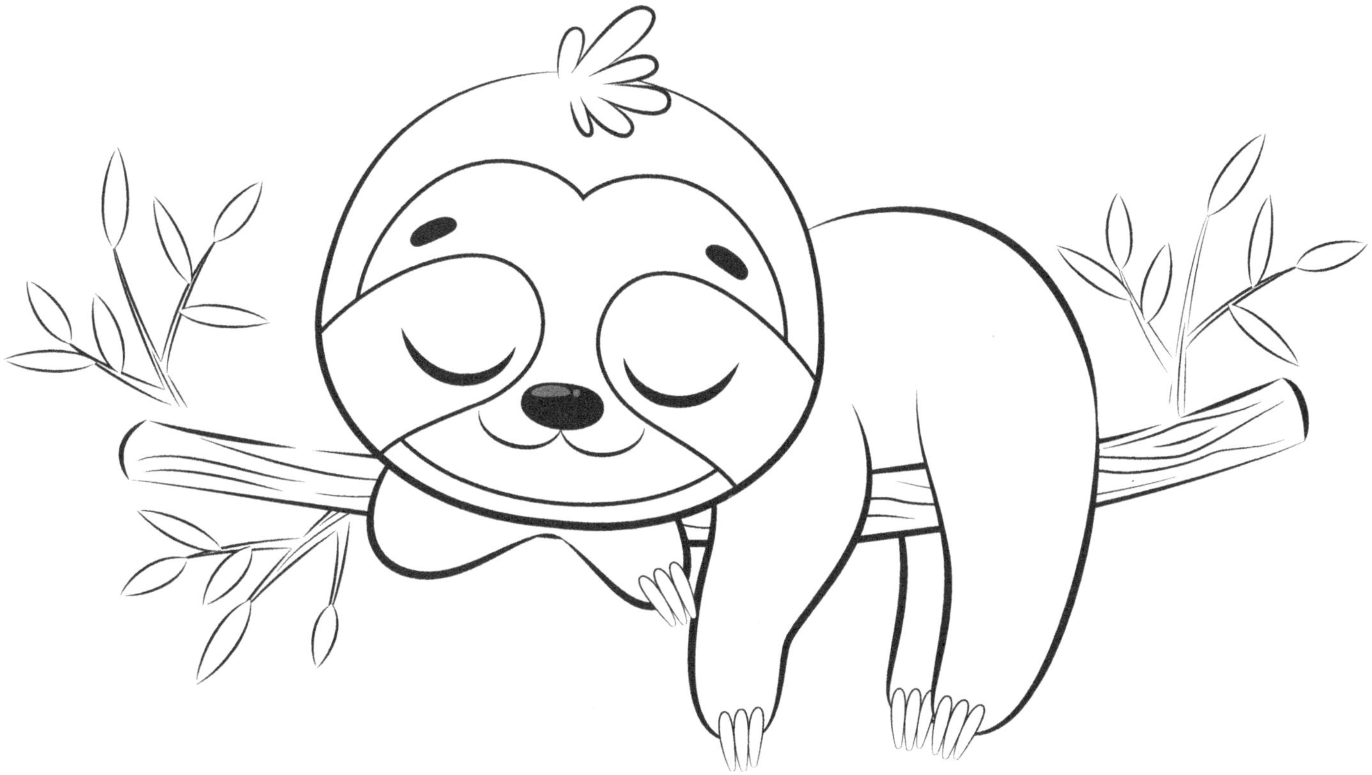

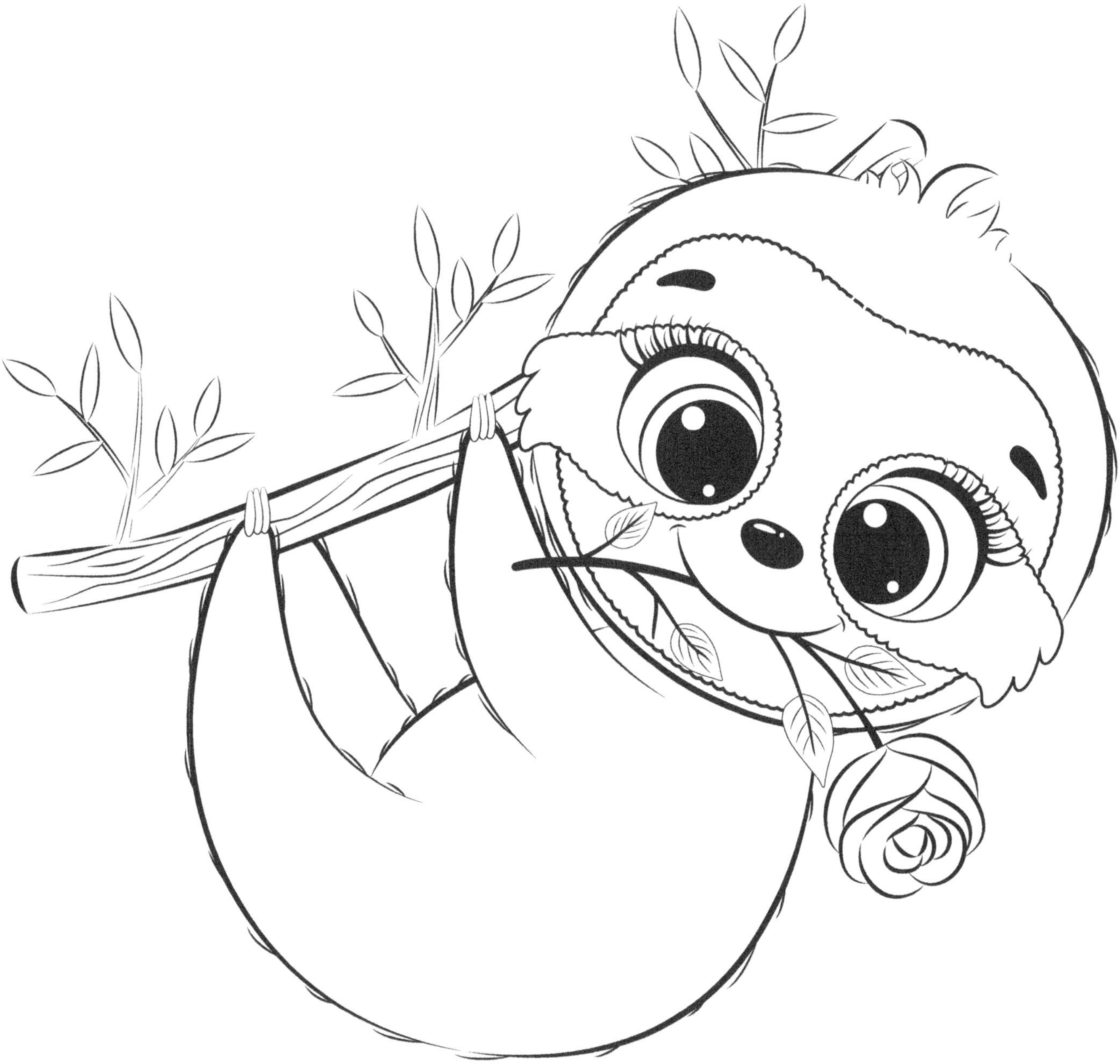

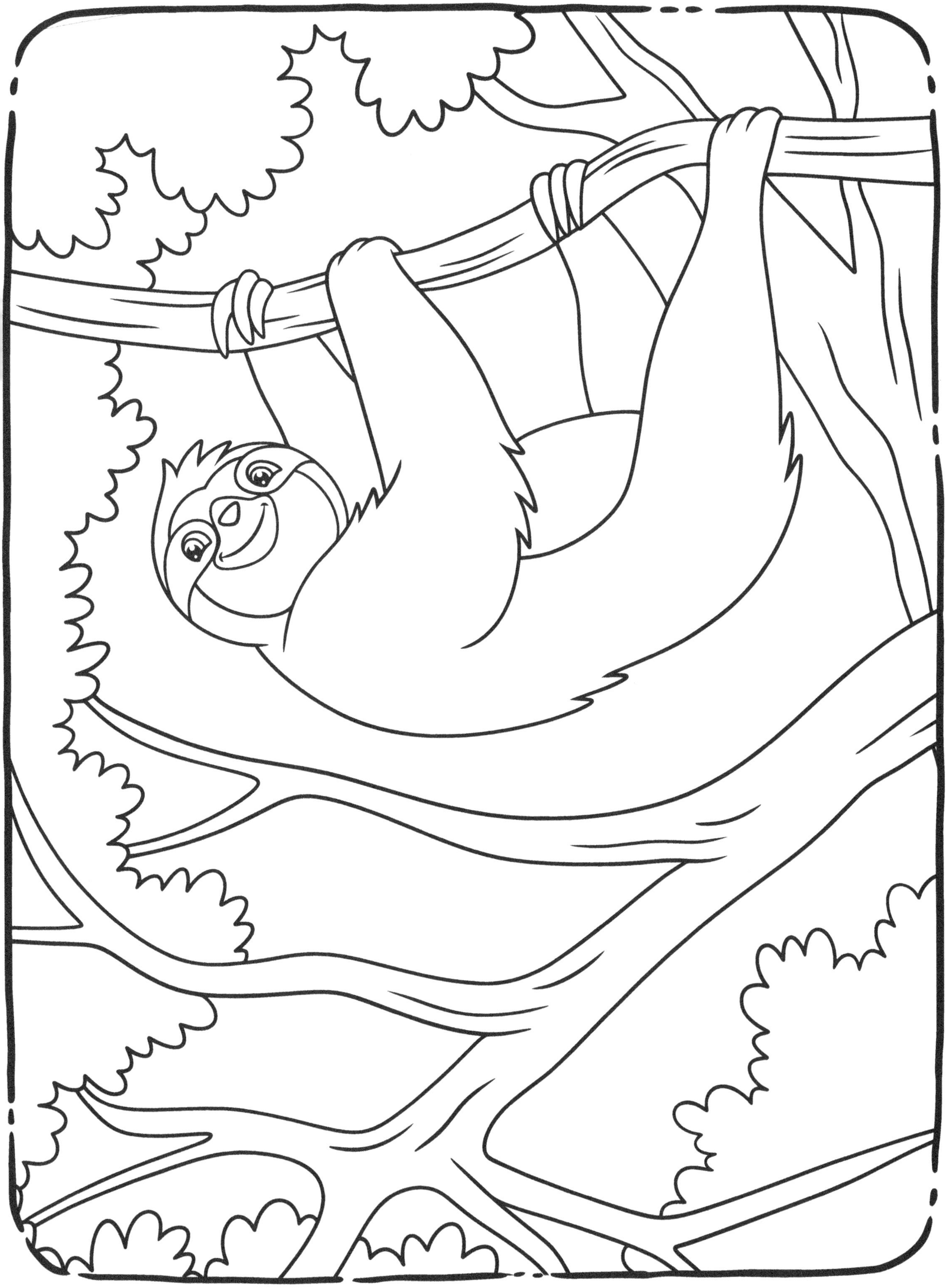

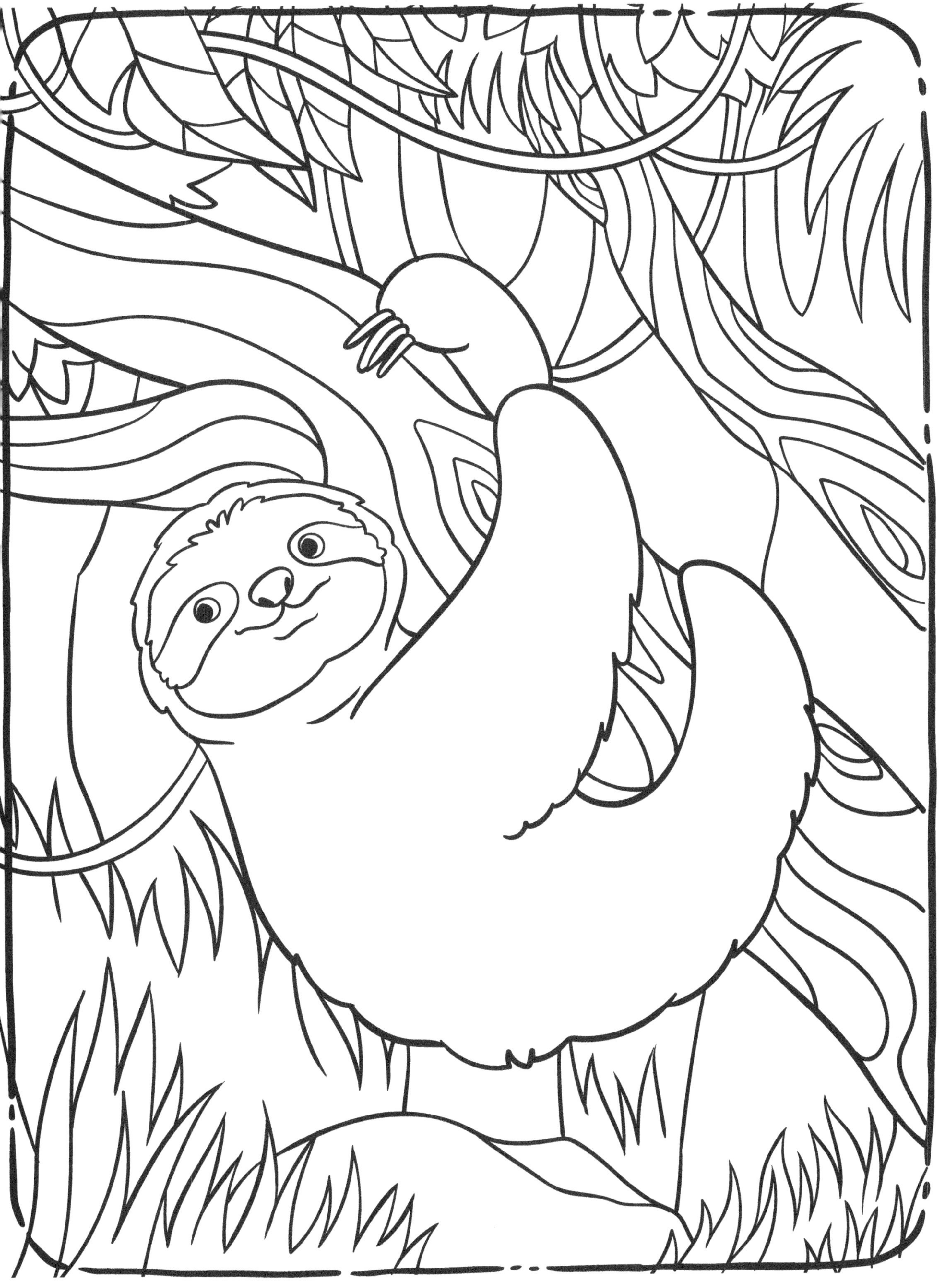

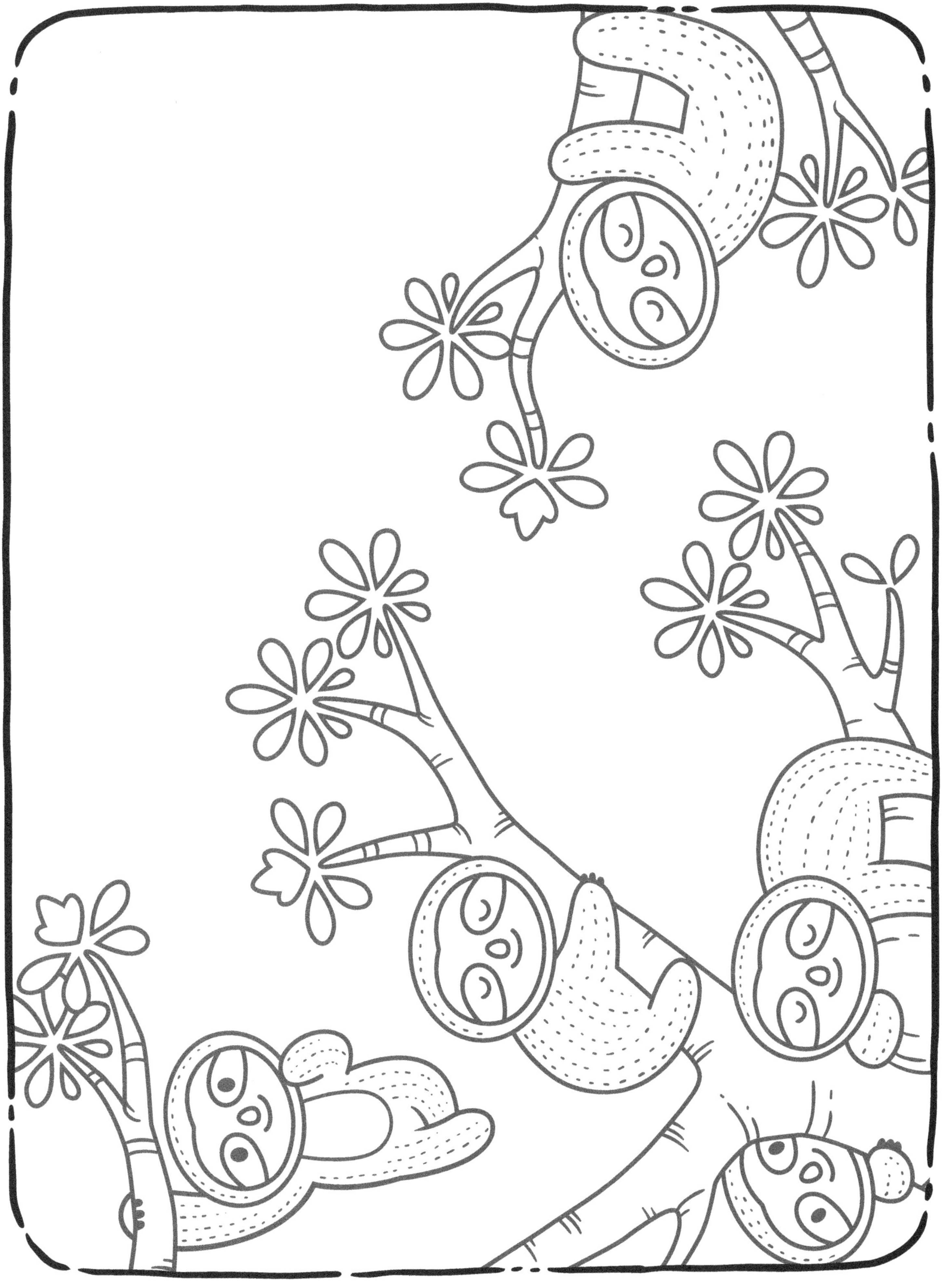

Made in United States
North Haven, CT
19 December 2024

63139110R00039